Learning in the Global Classroom

Learning in the Global Classroom

A Guide for Students in the Multicultural University

Carol Dalglish

Associate Professor, School of Management, Queensland University of Technology, Australia

Peter Evans

Principal, Leadership Education Australia

Lynda Lawson

Language and Learning Advisor, Queensland University of Technology, Australia

Edward Elgar
Cheltenham, UK • Northampton, MA, USA

Published by
Edward Elgar Publishing Limited
The Lypiatts
15 Lansdown Road
Cheltenham
Glos GL50 2JA
UK

Edward Elgar Publishing, Inc.
William Pratt House
9 Dewey Court
Northampton
Massachusetts 01060
USA

A catalogue record for this book
is available from the British Library

Library of Congress Control Number: 2010939202

ISBN 978 1 84844 869 8 (cased)

Typeset by Servis Filmsetting Ltd, Stockport, Cheshire
Printed and bound by MPG Books Group, UK

Contents

1	Introduction	1
2	The global classroom	10
3	Exchange and study abroad	20
4	Studying in a foreign culture	38
5	Benefiting from lectures	48
6	The challenges and skills of participation	58
7	Working in groups and teams	70
8	The case method: 'learning by doing'	80
9	Communication: writing in the global classroom	96
10	Communication: speaking in the global classroom	119
11	Success with assessment and examinations	135
12	Research students in the global classroom	149
Index		167

1. Introduction

I recommend that international students take advantage of all the services available to them such as tutors, learning support services, help from lecturers and so on. (Karolina – student, QUT, 2009)

As a student in a tertiary institution you will almost certainly be involved in what has become known as international education. This can happen in a number of ways. You may attend a class in your own home country or locality where you study alongside students from around the world. You may choose to gain your academic qualifications through studying in another country with an unfamiliar cultural and geographical context. You may have a study period abroad as part of your study programme. In today's globalized world you cannot avoid 'international' education. What is important is how to benefit from this experience whatever form it takes. And that is what this book is about.

International education around the world has grown exponentially in recent years. Tertiary education around the world now has an increasing mix of domestic and international students in classes. Many Western countries including the United States, the United Kingdom, Australia, New Zealand and Canada provide education for significant numbers of foreign students from an increasingly diverse range of countries. They teach in English and use a 'Western' educational philosophy. This can raise a number of issues for students whose first language is not English or who have experienced a different approach to education and the acquisition of knowledge.

Similar problems can arise when students from 'Western' countries choose to spend some part of their study period in a different culture. Both of these trends mean that any tertiary classroom is likely to be made up of people from very different backgrounds.

Below is a list of the countries which welcome the most international students and the top source countries for their international students in 2005:

- USA. The top five source countries are India, China, South Korea, Japan and Canada. These five countries make up 46 per cent of the foreign students studying in higher education in the USA.

- UK. The top five non-EU source countries are China, the USA, India, Malaysia and Hong Kong. These students make up 49 per cent of the non-EU foreign students.
- Australia. The top five source countries, are China, India, Malaysia, Hong Kong and Indonesia. These students make up 56 per cent of the total foreign students.
- Canada. The top five source countries include China, the USA, France, India and South Korea. They make up 46 per cent of foreign students studying in Canada.
- New Zealand. The top five source countries include China, South Korea, Japan, the USA and India. These make up 80 per cent of foreign student numbers in New Zealand (AEI.dest.gov.au/AEI/ Publications & Research n.d.).

As can be seen from the above figures, despite the overall diversity of countries whose citizens travel to study, these five primary English language destinations are drawing from many of the same source countries, in particular China and India where economic growth is still strong. Without considering the wide range of countries that make up the other '50 per cent', the diversity of culture, education systems and world-view apparent within these primary source countries is considerable.

If you are a student from one of these host countries you will meet up with students from around the world in your tertiary classroom. They may make you feel uncomfortable with their different approach or their slower spoken English. They are, however, a valuable resource for those of you who are not able to travel overseas as they bring the world, its perspectives and attitudes to you. Take the time to overcome the superficial barriers that language and culture present in the classroom. This book will help you.

About 1.6 million students study outside their home country every year and of those over 500 000 study in the US (Mazzarol and Hosie, cited in Avirutha et al. 2005). Education is the third-largest export in Australia (Marginson 2002), with over 100 000 foreign students studying at Australian universities in 2000. It is predicted that this number will rise to over 500 000 by 2020 (IDP 2002).

If you have chosen to study in one of these major Western providers of tertiary education, this book will help you understand the expectations often present in English language-based tertiary education. Things will be different, but this book will help you understand the processes used and how to do well within this system.

ADVANTAGES OF INTERNATIONAL EDUCATION

One of the primary advantages of studying abroad is to learn a new culture and adapt to a new learning environment through real-life experiences (Rhee and Danowitz Sagaria 2004; Avirutha et al. 2005). This is increasingly important whatever discipline you are studying as there is every chance that you will eventually work across a range of countries and cultures, or with people from a range of different backgrounds. Cross-cultural understanding will have an impact on your effectiveness as a professional in an increasingly global environment. Therefore, in the classroom you have the opportunity to learn not only from the lecturer but also from your fellow students, who may come from very different cultural backgrounds to yourself. In the classroom you have the opportunity of mixing with, and learning from, people who have experienced and understand places that have cultures very different from your own. This will offer new insights and new solutions to problems that would be difficult to acquire in a monocultural context.

It is important to remember that Australia, the USA, the United Kingdom and many of the other Western host countries of international students are themselves extremely culturally diverse communities, but that tertiary education remains essentially monocultural in form and Anglo-American in content (De Cieri and Olekalns 2001). That means there are particular philosophies that put an emphasis on student autonomy, on participatory teaching and learning strategies and content from a 'Western' perspective. This may not be what you have experienced in the past. If you are a student undertaking study abroad, particularly in a non-Western education system, you may be equally challenged by the different processes you experience there. There is a special chapter in the book (Chapter 3) on studying abroad and adjusting to cultural difference in a very short space of time (for example one semester).

It is not always possible to travel abroad for your education. In these circumstances it is even more important to learn from those around you. The term 'internationalization at home' has been coined for a phenomenon defined as: 'The process of integrating an international dimension into the research, teaching and services function of higher education' (Knight 1993).

This definition does not inform us of how this process occurs in different universities. The term 'internationalization at home' has not caught on, but the process of internationalizing the curriculum, services and reach of the university has grown at a great pace. The increase in international competition for students has driven this process of internationalization. It is important that tertiary institutions provide for all their students. But there has also been an increasing realization that all students will need to understand more about the global environment and different cultural practices and attitudes if they are to be successful in an increasingly global world.

CHALLENGES OF INTERNATIONAL EDUCATION

Many of you who study in Western universities may want to understand the 'Western' way of doing things, but may not be familiar or comfortable with the processes used to facilitate learning (Pincas 2001). Business classrooms traditionally use a range of Western teaching and learning strategies that focus on critical analysis, oral discussion, problem-solving and the possibility of multiple solutions, using case studies and discussion groups that require active participation by the students, which many international students find unfamiliar. Many of the chapters of this book will address how you can develop the skills necessary to benefit from these ways of teaching and learning.

You all come to the tertiary classroom with a set of behaviours and characteristics that make you unique (Jones 2005). You have your own expectations arising from the educational practices of your home communities. It is important for you to think about what it is you are hoping to learn. Why have you chosen to attend the particular institution you are enrolled with? Are you looking to learn a foreign language? Do you want to use your newly acquired skills in your own country, in the country in which you are studying, or somewhere else? Understanding exactly what it is you want to achieve can greatly help you get the best out of the international experience both within and without the classroom.

REFLECTION

Think about what you would like to know about other countries, perhaps ones that you hope to work in or visit. Other students around you may have similar aspirations. You are an 'expert' on your locality so you have very valuable information and understanding to share. Be willing to share it. You may be the only person in your class with your particular ethnic, cultural or national background. This is valuable.

In classrooms with students from Europe, North and South America, Asia, India, Africa and Australia, the potential for intercultural understanding and skills development is enormous. But it won't happen by accident. You need to make opportunities to mix with students from other countries. If you belong to the host community, ask international students to join in your activities outside of the university. If you are the visiting student, find the courage to get to know your host community. It can seem very difficult, particularly if you do not share a common language, but it is worth the effort.

UNDERSTANDING THE LEARNING PROCESS

Each of us, wherever we come from, has our preferred way of learning. We have had our preference reinforced by the methods used in our home countries, but equally you may find that the different teaching and learning methods you face, whilst a little daunting to start with, help you learn well.

According to the visual–auditory–kinaesthetic learning style model (VAK), most people possess a dominant or preferred learning style; however, some people have a mixed and evenly balanced blend of the three styles. This model provides a very easy and quick reference inventory to help you understand your preferred learning style and help you choose learning experiences that will be positive for you. It will also help you understand that different people learn differently, and therefore many different teaching and learning practices might be used in the classroom.

- A visual learning style means that you may learn more quickly through the use of seen or observed things, including pictures, diagrams, demonstrations, displays, handouts, films, flip-charts, and so on.
- An auditory learning style means that you like to learn through listening: to the spoken word, to self or others, to sounds and noises.
- A kinaesthetic learning style means that you learn best through physical experience: touching, feeling, holding, doing, practical hands-on experiences.

Below is a simple test to help you assess your preferred learning style. It is simply an indicator of preferred learning styles.

VAK Self-Assessment

Score each statement in Table 1.1 and then add the totals for each column to indicate your learning style dominance and mix. Your learning style is

Table 1.1   VAK self-assessment

		A	B	C
1	When operating new equipment for the first time I prefer to . . .	Read the instructions	Listen to or ask for an explanation	Have a go and learn by 'trial and error'
2	When seeking travel directions I . . .	Look at a map	Ask for directions	Follow my nose or maybe use a compass
3	When cooking a new dish I . . .	Follow a recipe	Call a friend for explanation	Follow my instinct, tasting as I cook
4	I tend to say . . .	'I see what you mean'	'I hear what you are saying'	'I know how you feel'
5	I tend to say . . .	'Show me'	'Tell me'	'Let me try'
6	I prefer these leisure activities:	Museums or galleries	Music or conversation	Physical activities or making things
7	Choosing a holiday I . . .	Read the brochures	Listen to recommendations	Imagine the experience
8	Choosing a new car I . . .	Read the reviews	Discuss with friends	Test-drive what I fancy
9	Learning a new skill I . . .	Watch what the teacher is doing	Talk through with the teacher exactly what I am supposed to do	Work it out as I go along by doing it
10	I remember things best by . . .	Writing notes or keeping printed details	Saying them aloud or repeating words and key points in my head or listening to a recording	Doing and practising the activity, or imagining it being done
11	I feel especially connected to others because of . . .	How they look	What they say to me	How they make me feel
12	When I revise for an exam, I . . .	Write lots of revision notes	Talk over the material with other people	Imagine the answer
13	When explaining something to someone, I tend to . . .	Show them what I mean	Explain to them in different ways until they understand	Encourage them to try
14	My main interests are:	Photography, reading, watching films or people-watching	Listening to music or listening to the radio or talking to friends	Physical/sports activities, or fine wines, fine foods or dancing
15	I find it easiest to remember . . .	Faces	Names	What I was doing
	Totals			

Source: Adapted from Victoria Chislett MSc and Alan Chapman 2005.

also a reflection of the type of person you are – how you perceive things and the way that you relate to the world. This questionnaire helps you to improve your understanding of yourself and your strengths. There are no right or wrong answers.

Add up your scores. Column A shows a visual preference, Column B an auditory preference and column C a kinaesthetic preference. The higher your score, the greater your preference for this means of learning.

This is only a quick quiz but can help you understand what you need to do to help you earn. It is rough guide only. It can also help you understand others who you work and learn with.

STRUCTURE OF THE BOOK

This book is aimed at three groups of tertiary students and those who help them to learn.

Group One is students from around the world who engage in cross-border education in one of the many English-speaking nations who encourage participation by international students. They are generally referred to as international students and study outside their home country for an extended period of time – usually a year or more. It is assumed that these students will be studying in a Western-oriented institution where English is the language of instruction.

Group Two is students from Western English-speaking nations who choose to do part of their study in a different cultural and geographical location. They are generally referred to as study abroad or exchange students.

Group Three is students who are studying in English-speaking classrooms in their own countries and are joined by fellow students from a range of linguistic and cultural backgrounds. They are frequently referred to as domestic students.

The book provides a theoretical background to intercultural teaching and learning and provides suggestions and examples of how to be successful in the global business classroom. It starts by providing examples of the issues that arise when there are linguistic and cultural differences in the classroom; when expectations may be different and the impact of culture, both in and out of the classroom, on learning may be significant. It explores the different teaching and learning challenges that arise in a Western classroom and offers suggestions for getting the best out of the methods used. Each chapter will provide examples of the ideas discussed, comments from past students and practical exercises that will help you improve your learning outcomes.

REMEMBER:

'You learn from foreigners that there is more than one path to a goal. Effective wealth creation demands that we use all the paths available to us.' (Hampden-Turner and Trompenaars 1993: 16, cited in Sinclair and Wilson 1999: 27)

REFERENCES AND FURTHER READING

AEI.dest.gov.au/AEI/Publications & Research (n.d.), 'International Student Numbers'. Accessed July 2006.

Anderson, Mary (2001), *Cross-cultural Communication in the Global Classroom: Issues and Implications*, Melbourne: Monash University.

Avirutha, Anupong, Mai X. Bui, Geraldine H. Goodstone and Kenya Reid (2005), 'Current overview and future of business higher education', *Futurics*, **29** (1–2).

Ballard, Brigid and John Clanchy (1997), *Teaching International Students*, Sydney: IDP Education Australia.

Chislett, Victoria and Alan Chapman (2005), VAK learning styles self-test, http://www.businessballs.com/vaklearningstylestest.htm.

Coyne, David (2003), 'Internationalisation at home and the changing landscape', Internationalisation at Home Conference, Malmo University, April.

Cox, Taylor H. and Stacy Blake (1991), 'Managing cultural diversity: implications for organisational competitiveness', *Academy of Management Executive*, **5** (3).

Cunningham, Donna J. (2005), 'Teaching multiculturalism in an age of terrorism: a business perspective', *Cross Cultural Management*, **12** (2).

Dalglish, C. (1989), *Refugees from Vietnam*, Basingstoke: Macmillan

De Cieri, Helen and Mara Olekalns (2001), *Workforce Diversity in Australia: Challenges and Strategies for Diversity Management*, Melbourne: Monash University.

DomNwachukwu, Chinaka S. (2005), 'Standards-based planning and teaching in a multicultural classroom', *Multicultural Education*, **13** (1).

Hampden-Turner, C. and A. Trompenaars (1993), *The Seven Cultures of Capitalism*, New York: Doubleday.

Harding, S. (2004), *International at QUT*, QUT internal document, June 2004.

IDP Education Australia (2002), *Global Student Mobility*, Sydney: IDP.

Jacob, E.J. and John W. Greggo (2001), 'Using counsellor training and collaborative programming strategies in working with international students', *Journal of Multicultural Counselling and Development*, **29** (1), 29–34.

Jones, Lisa A. (2005), 'The cultural identity of students: what teachers should know', *Kappa Delta Pi Record*, **41** (4).

Knight, J. (1993), 'Internationalisation: management strategies and issues', *International Education Magazine*, Ottawa: CBIE.

Marginson, Simon (2002), 'The phenomenal rise of international degrees down under', *Change*, **34** (3), 34–43.

Nahal, Anita (2005), 'Cultural collisions', *Diverse Issues in Higher Education*, **22** (20)

Pincas, Anita (2001), 'Culture, cognition and communication in global education', *Distance Education*, **22** (1), 30–51.

QUT (2009), Issuport.qut.edu.au/language/what students/karolina.jsp?view.

Roosevelt, Thomas R. Jnr. (1996), *Redefining Diversity*, New York: American Management Association.

Rhee, Jeong-eun and Mary Ann Danowitz Sagaria (2004), 'International Students: constructions of imperialism in the Chronicles of Higher Education', *The Review of Higher Education*, **28** (1), 77–96.

Ryan, Janette (2000), *A Guide to Teaching International Students*, Oxford: OCSLD.

Sandstrom, Shirin (2003), 'Networking for internationalisation at home in nursing education', Internationalisation at Home Conference, Malmo University, April.

Sturz, Dominick and Brian H. Kleiner (2005), 'Effective management of cultural diversity in a classroom setting', *Equal Opportunities International*, **24** (5–6), 6–9.

Sinclair, Amanda and Valerie Britton Wilson (1999), *The Culture-Inclusive Classroom*, Melbourne: Melbourne Business School the University of Melbourne.

www.efmd.org/html/Accreditations: Accessed July 2006.

2. The global classroom

A fish only discovers its need for water when it is no longer in it. Our own culture is like water to a fish. It sustains us. We live and breathe through it. (Trompenaars and Hampden-Turner 2002: 20)

MEANING OF CULTURE AND ITS IMPACT

Culture will be explored from two perspectives. In this chapter we will define culture and explore the impact it has in the classroom. Chapter 4 will look more broadly at living in a different culture and the possible impact this will have on your studies, and the strategies you can employ to respond positively to a new environment.

We take culture so much for granted that it is difficult to define. Using Ed Schein's (1985) definition of culture as the starting point, we define culture as: a set of basic assumptions, shared solutions to universal problems of external adaptation (how to survive in the external environment) and internal integration (how to stay together as a community), which have evolved over time and are handed down from one generation to another. There are number of layers to culture, which is why the word means so many different things to different people. There is the external appearance – the outer layer – the explicit products (Trompenaars and Hampden-Turner 2002) or, as Schein (1985) calls it, the artefact level. An individual's first experience of a new culture is the explicit culture.

Explicit culture is the observable reality of the language, food, buildings, dress, arts and festivals. They are symbols of a deeper level of culture. Prejudices mostly start on this symbolic and observable level. It is easy to place an inappropriate cultural meaning on new behaviours. The same behaviour may mean different things in different cultures.

One of the most difficult questions for someone to answer about their own culture is: why do you do that? The explicit culture that is observed reflects the norms and values of that particular cultural group. Norms are the mutual sense a group has of what is 'right' and 'wrong'.

ACTIVITY

Identify three norms from your own culture – this may be easiest to do by identifying particular behaviour such as dress or greetings – and identify what that is meant to say about the society. What do these behaviours reflect about the culture? This may be as simple as how you greet a stranger, or an important person or your friend. How is this done differently, and why do you greet in this way? What does it tell you about what your society believes?

Values determine the definition of good or bad and are therefore closely associated with the ideals the group shares. For example the value of modesty in Islam is reflected in the mode of dress recommended. Norms provide a framework for how you should behave, and values give us the ideal behaviour. So values help you decide between alternative behaviours.

When you want to ask a question in class, think about how your values affect whether and how you do this. If you are reluctant to ask questions, ask yourself why. Is it because you are shy of strangers? Is it because in your society it would be considered bad manners to challenge a teacher in the class? Compare what you think with those around you, and how they behave. What does the teacher ask you to do? If you don't understand why you are required to take a particular action, ask. Email and private interviews mean that you can do this without embarrassing either yourself or the teacher.

People may behave as expected in a society because other people do – or because they share the values that underpin the norm. When shared meanings of norms and values are stable and seen to be relevant to the group's situation, a cultural tradition develops.

But there is yet another layer to culture, and that is the core assumptions about existence that underlie the norms and values. The most basic value that people strive for is survival. In different parts of the world different behaviours have developed because of the different circumstances in which people find themselves and the different challenges they face to survive. Over time we do not challenge the assumptions that have led to our particular cultural behaviour, so trying to explore this can be both difficult and revealing.

Think of two questions. Ask those who come from a hierarchical society, such as Japan, why they respect authority. Ask why people in Australia are equal. You will find this leads to some discomfort, and if taken seriously, to hard reflection. Understanding these underlying assumptions about existence can explain a great many of the values and norms that different societies have – and the fact that the conditions of survival have changed doesn't necessarily mean that the norms and values change.

Culture directs our actions. Culture is man-made, confirmed by others, conventionalized and passed on over time. It provides a meaningful context in which to meet, to think about ourselves, and face the outer world (Trompenaars and Hampden-Turner 2002). These are all taken for granted until we meet with people who have developed a very different way of doing these things. Culture is developed by people interacting and determining further action, so it is always changing.

Kluckhohn and Strodtbeck (1961) argue that humanity is confronted with universally shared problems emerging from relationships with others, time, activity and nature. One culture can be distinguished from another by the solutions it chooses. The solutions depend on the meaning given by people to life in general and to other people, time and nature in particular.

Despite the growing similarities at the artefact level of culture, as communication and travel appear to make the world smaller, it would be misleading to believe that therefore we are all becoming more alike. The advent of the European Union did not reduce the differences between the French and the Germans in how they go about problem-solving. It may be that with the pressure for integration, the process of globalization is creating an equal if not stronger pressure for divergence as a statement of difference, as a reflection of the deeper levels of culture (Kluckhohn and Strodtbeck 1961; Triandis 1972).

Each student and teacher brings to the learning situation the values and attitudes of their culture. Many of the core values are assumed to be shared by others because they are the fundamentals of the way of life; they are seldom talked about, let alone discussed or challenged. It is these often unacknowledged assumptions that create miscommunication and impair learning in the global classroom.

The values embedded in a culture influence the behaviour of teachers and students as well as their reaction to each other and the learning environment. Trompenaars and Hampden-Turner (2002) provide a framework of five dimensions of culture which impact on the nature of the student–teacher relationship. You need to identify where you sit on the dimensions to be discussed. This will help you understand your expectations. These dimensions will also give you a framework for understanding what is happening in the classroom and with your fellow students.

UNIVERSALISM VERSUS PARTICULARISM (RULES VERSUS RELATIONSHIPS)

The universalist approach is that what is good and right can be defined, is embedded in rules, and always applies. In a particularist culture greater attention is paid to obligation and relationship, and less to abstract rules.

In the classroom a universalist teacher will focus more on rules than relationships. There will be a clearly defined statement of mutual obligations and rules to be abided by and these rules must be obeyed. An example might be that there are clear guidelines about the penalty for the late submission of work. This penalty is laid out very specifically and applied to everyone who submits late.

The particularist teacher will focus more on relationships, and the rules can be changed in response to the changing nature of circumstances for each individual. In a universalist world this is not considered fair.

Think about your previous experiences in the classroom. What was the prevailing attitude? Was there a focus on rules or relationships? What is the prevailing view in the current classroom situation?

There is no point in seeing either of these ways as right or wrong. You need to identify which is prevailing in the classroom and try to understand what this means for you as a student.

COMMUNITARIANISM VERSUS INDIVIDUALISM (THE GROUP VERSUS THE INDIVIDUAL)

With an individualist approach the focus is on the individual, and they have freedom to contribute as they see fit. The communitarian perspective considers the community first. Individualistic cultures make frequent use of the 'I' form and people are seen to achieve alone and assume personal responsibility.

In communitarian cultures the use of 'we' is more frequent. People ideally achieve in groups, and assume group responsibility. In the learning context the teacher and the learners are equally responsible for the student's success.

Many global classrooms include activities that reflect both attitudes, and students from different cultural backgrounds will find difficult the activities that do not reflect their cultural preference. For example, if you come from an individualistic culture you may find it difficult to work as a team member where the group outcome is more important than your individual contribution. If you are used to working as part of a group you may feel isolated and vulnerable when you are expected to perform on your own and are praised as an individual.

Classrooms will include students from both cultural approaches. Recognize them and work as well as you can to adapt to the perspective required. Understand that others are also finding it difficult.

NEUTRAL VERSUS EMOTIONAL (THE RANGE OF FEELINGS EXPRESSED)

Should the nature of our interactions in the classroom be objective and detached, or is expressing emotion acceptable? You may well have an instant reaction to what you think is appropriate in a public classroom.

In neutral cultures relationships in class are generally instrumental and about achieving objectives. There is a very limited relationship between the teacher and the students, and everyone is expected to work in a very task-oriented way. In more emotional cultures, the expression of emotion is acceptable. In the classroom, members of neutral cultures express themselves by behaving in a cool, self-possessed manner with personal feelings not demonstrated. In more culturally emotional contexts, thoughts and feelings are revealed verbally and non-verbally. Touching, gesturing and strong facial expressions are common.

Think about the normal emotional responses in your culture. Is it acceptable to show emotions in public? How much? When?

DIFFUSE VERSUS SPECIFIC (THE RANGE OF INVOLVEMENT)

When the whole person is involved in the teaching–learning relationship there is real personal contact between individuals, instead of the relationship being determined by the specifics of the role of teacher and student. In many cultures diffused relationships are not only preferred but necessary, and there is an assumption that there is a complex relationship between teacher and student that extends beyond the delivery of subject expertise. In a culture that values specificity, principles and consistent moral standards are independent of the person being addressed. That is, the teacher is unlikely to make allowance for, or even know about, individual circumstances. The relationship is specific to the teaching–learning situation. In diffuse cultures morality is situationally dependent on the person and the context, and extenuating circumstances are accepted as the norm.

ACHIEVEMENT VERSUS ASCRIPTION (HOW STATUS IS ACCORDED)

An achievement orientation means that you are judged on what you have achieved. In this situation students are seen to be equal irrespective of their social backgrounds, and their status changes as they achieve high grades for example.

Ascription means that status is attributed to you as a result of birth, age, educational level, connections and so on. In the achievement-oriented classroom titles are only used when relevant to the task. Respect for the teacher is based on how effective he or she is and how much he or she has achieved. In ascription-oriented cultures there is extensive use of title to clarify status. Respect for the teacher is seen as a measure of the students' commitment to learning and the university they attended.

Think about the culture that you come from. Is greater emphasis put on what people have achieved, or the strata of society that they come from?

It is important to remember that the classroom is likely to run along lines in sympathy with the prevailing culture in which you are studying. This may be very different from your own. You need to be aware of what is expected of you so that you can modify your behaviour to do well in the new situation. You do not have to change your beliefs – you simply have to acknowledge difference.

TEACHING AND LEARNING EXPECTATIONS

When you enter a new classroom, reflect back on the last classroom you were part of. How did it work? What was the size? What teaching methods were used? Were you expected to be passive, or to participate? These are the circumstances under which you have been successful. Do not assume that your new classroom will work in the same way. The first thing to discover is what the new expectations are.

Here we provide an oversight of what to expect in a Western English language-based classroom. There is a chapter looking at each of the different teaching methods you may be confronted with. Expect difference. There will be difference because you are now studying at a different level, you are studying at a different institution and your classmates and teachers may come from very different cultural backgrounds. Try to work out what your assumptions are, so that you can ask the questions necessary to find out what the assumptions are in this new situation.

You may not be used to participating in class discussion – this can be assumed by the teacher to mean that you are not engaged, do not understand or are not interested. Patterns of behaviour like learning by rote, and replicating the answers you are given, will be challenged. This is not the usual way 'Western' classes work. It can be a challenge to recognize that you have to show that you know the content you have been taught, or read, that you acknowledge the source accurately, and then you have to express an opinion.

If you are working in a group, you may find different group members have very different ideas about participation and how to work as a member of a group. There is a potential for misunderstanding and it is always useful to share with your group member what your previous educational experiences have been and to clarify what is expected.

Different types of classroom activities are covered in the different chapters of this book so that you can prepare to get the best out of whatever practices your institution uses, whatever the patterns were in your past.

RELATIONSHIPS WITH TEACHERS

Think about your teachers in your previous institution. How did you address your teacher? What did you expect from your teacher? What did the teacher expect from you? As you saw in the previous section, relationships between teachers and students can vary greatly from one cultural context to the next. This is not a reflection of a lack of respect for teachers, but a reflection of the cultural values that exist in that community.

In some cultures the teacher is the 'expert', there to provide guidance and technical expertise, but not likely to become personally involved with any of the students. In other cultures the relationship is one of mentor, taking a personal interst in the achievements of the students and perhaps even having a relationship outside of the classroom. In some cultures teachers are remote figures who cannot be approached. In other cultures they are very approachable, addressed by their personal names.

Many cultures have a high level of respect for teachers. As a result, teachers are seldom if ever challenged. You may think that even to ask questions suggests that the lecturer is not being effective:

> If a lecturer does not answer a student's question in class but asks their students what they think, in my country we would think that the teacher is either poorly qualified or lazy. But in Australia this way of not giving an answer . . . it is common in our class even when the Professor is our teacher. (Third-year Thai student, Ballard and Clanchy 1997: 15)

> The other students ask many questions and even argue with the professor. I could never do that, because I do not think it is right behaviour. I do not want

to become like Australian students. (Second-year Thai undergraduate, Ballard and Clanchy 1997: 15)

It is also true that in some cultures the achievement of the students is seen to be a shared responsibility between the student and the teacher. The idea most prevalent in the West is that learning is entirely the responsibility of the student, that there is no relationship between teacher and student. This is not always easy to understand. Great emphasis is put on self-directed learning. In Taiwan for example, students expressed their desire for achievement by stating that they would be the best students I (the teacher) had ever had. They clearly saw a relationship between their achievement and my status as a teacher (Dalglish and Evans 2008: 12). This is unlikely to happen in an Australian classroom.

LANGUAGE AND COMMUNICATION

Language is often held up as one of the most difficult challenges in the global classroom. Studying in a language that is not your mother tongue has many challenges. There are challenges for both the international student and the domestic student in that both may have difficulty understanding the accents of other speakers. Foreign students may have great difficulty with the English dialects they may come across, for example in the UK – many of which do not greatly resemble the English they learnt at language school. Domestic students may find the accents of non-native speakers difficult to understand. Patience and respect are required in both cases. The way you speak English is not necessarily a reflection of your understanding, but clear English is critical to you being understood.

Whether you are a non-native English speaker or a native speaker it is important to understand that the following difficulties are likely to occur in your learning situation:

- You may need more thinking time, particularly if you are not fluent and are still translating. This thinking time may not always be available, so prepare before class so that you have thought through anything you may be asked.
- Some concepts may be difficult to translate. For example, if you live in a country that does not have a 'social security' system then trying to understand what is being said can be difficult. Learn as much as you can about the culture in which you are studying. Ask questions. Read newspapers and listen to the media. This will not only provide

good contextual knowledge, but also improve your ability to listen, read and speak more fluently.

- Listening and speaking can both present challenges. You may find that you have a range of lecturers with different accents, so understanding what they are saying can be difficult even if you could read about the subject quite easily. Be prepare to use audio-visual materials to help you understand. See if you can record the lecture so that you have a chance to listen again, and seek help if you still don't understand.

- Most subjects sit in a very specific culture. Each discipline has its own language which may be quite different to 'ordinary' language. Each discipline has its own vocabulary that will not have been included in your English classes. Also, many subjects may draw on the history and culture of the host country, referring to incidents and practices that may be quite unfamiliar to you. Making friends with someone from the host culture can help you understand these context-specific statements; but if they are central to the subject you need to ask the teacher to explain.

- In-depth understanding of local culture and norms is often taken for granted in the classroom. There is a risk that different words mean different things in different national cultures so that both you and the teacher understand what is being said – but your understanding is different. If in doubt, ask.

  Example: A Vietnamese man in a language class, who worked in a factory during the day, had been told by a colleague to make a good impression on the supervisor. He did not know what the word 'impression' meant, so looked it up. The definition he found in the dictionary was 'to make a mark with a heavy implement'. He was sensible enough to assume that this was not what his colleague meant – so he asked.

- Remember, slow speech does not mean slow brain. Fast speech, or a lot of speech, does not mean that the speaker is smart.

REFERENCES

Ballard, B. and J. Clanchy (1997), *Teaching International Students*, Melbourne: IDP Education Australia.

Dalglish, C. and P. Evans (2008), *Teaching in the Global Business Classroom*, Cheltenham, UK and Northampton, MA, USA: Edward Elgar Publishing.

Kluckhohn, F. and F. Strodtbeck (1961), *Variations in Value Orientations*, Evanston, IL: Greenwood Press.

Schein, E.H. (1985), *Organisational Culture and Leadership*, San Francisco, CA: Jossey-Bass.

Triandis, H.C. (1972), *The Analysis of Subjective Culture*, New York: Wiley Interscience.

Trompenaars, F. and C. Hampden Turner (2002), *Riding the Waves of Culture* (2nd edition), London: Nicholas Brearley.

3. Exchange and study abroad*

STUDY ABROAD: THE MOST CHALLENGING AND REWARDING YEAR OF YOUR LIFE

> I can honestly say that my life has been shaped and reshaped by my year abroad
> ... without the experience I would never have taken the roads and detours that
> have led to such a fascinating life and career. (Study abroad participant, cited
> in Norris and Gillespie 2008)

This chapter is designed primarily for English-speaking students who are planning to do some part of their study time in another country. It incorporates the words of a number of students who have studied abroad.

It will look at some reasons why you should study abroad; decisions you will need to make about where to go; preparation and leaving; issues you will face during your time abroad, for example homesickness; different study styles; and returning home. Some points about working abroad and some useful links will be given in the final section.

WHY STUDY ABROAD?

> There are only so many times you can analyse globalization without going
> abroad yourself. (Australian exchange student to Japan)

There is a huge push to involve students in study abroad. Governments have recognized the benefits for their people. In the USA the Simon Bill, passed in 2009, aims to have 1 million US students study abroad by 2020 (http://www.nafsa.org/press_releases). In Europe, the aim is to have 3 million students involved in international study by 2012 (Loveland 2008). Scholarships for international study are also available in Australia, Canada, New Zealand and many other countries. Why is this the case?

BECOMING A CONFIDENT GLOBAL CITIZEN

If you spend some time studying abroad as part of your degree or undertake an internship in another country, it is an opportunity to learn from the global community and step toward becoming a global citizen, and to challenge your own ways of thinking. You may have an opportunity to learn a new language; you will learn to communicate across cultures and how to get along with those from different backgrounds. Your people skills and teamwork skills will be enhanced. Returning students also expressed an increased empathy for minorities, having been in the minority themselves, and now viewed themselves as participants in a world community (Barribal et al. 2008).

You will develop independence and confidence through planning your trip and your study. In fact research suggest that being able to make decisions on your own is key to successful study abroad (Hadis 2005). Your personal resourcefulness and resilience will be tested and developed when you make those plans happen, and have to deal with unexpected developments and living and studying in a new environment. Many students report making friends who remain so for life.

YOUR STUDIES

> I was halfway through my course and I was getting tempted to drop out . . . my lecturer told me I would be mad if I didn't take the opportunity to study in Japan for six months. (Australian Study Abroad student)

Study abroad can be a huge boost to your studies. It can remotivate you when you may be feeling like dropping out, and a number of studies suggest that students who have studied abroad perform better in their final year and come back with more motivation and career focus (Mcormack et al. 2008; Hadis 2005). For example, nurses who had studied abroad returned with increased cultural sensitivity, increased nursing knowledge and a global perspective on nursing (Barribal et al. 2008). Students report coming back with more confidence in themselves and in their ability to handle challenges.

FUTURE CAREER

Study abroad can have a major impact on your career. In a survey of over 17 000 study abroad participants in the USA, a large number reported that it had ignited interest in the career direction they had pursued, and that through it they had acquired skills that influenced their career path (Norris and Gillespie 2008). Study abroad can provide globally transferable skills, greater employability, improved global knowledge and language skills. To put it another way, study abroad is good for your resume.

Many employers are also interested in the personal skills and resourcefulness you used to survive on your own abroad. Casey, an Australian who spent one year studying international business in France, found this to be the case:

> On return, my first serious job interview was for a management consultancy position . . . after the usual questions the rest of the interview was mostly about the time I had spent in France . . . they were really interested in what strategies I used to live abroad . . . had joined a local cycling club and followed the Tour de France; they were really interested in that. I got the job.

The career impact of study abroad is much greater for those who have worked internationally, have participated in an internship, have studied abroad for a full year, have host university course enrolment and have lived with a host family (Norris and Gillespie 2008). Consider these factors when making decisions about study abroad if you want to maximize all the career benefits from your stay.

DECISIONS

Where To Go?

> Going and studying is like living there, you are not . . . just travelling. I advise anyone to do it. (Australian exchange student)

A huge range of study options are available – your first port of call should be the study abroad office at your university to see which other universities your home campus has signed agreements with. Some universities offer a certificate to recognize your study abroad, for example the Macquarie University Study Abroad Certificate in Sydney, Australia. This could be useful for your resume; check out how your time abroad will be acknowledged. Your choice of destination will also be determined by your personal culture, perhaps your ethnic background, the area of study you are interested in, maybe a long-held passion to visit a particular area. The range of opportunities is broad. For example Seton Hall in the USA has had a summer programme in Cairo for many years where students may undertake studies in Islamic jurisprudence and international human rights (Tobenkin 2009).

You may wish to undertake a service to others, for example as an engineering student, a teacher or a health professional. There are many opportunities to do this. See the section on internships at the end of the chapter for examples. Along with your personal motivation which will keep your study abroad dream alive, you will also need to consider the following questions.

How Far Out of My Comfort Zone am I Able to Go at this Stage of My Life?

There is likely to be more stress on you personally in a country where the language and culture are very different. So weigh up whether you are ready for the challenge and how much you are really committed to study in a particular area.

How Long Can I Go For?

A month is more of a study tour; you will probably go in a group and while this will be a great introduction to a country, a longer stay of six months or a year will give you greater insight and language skills. A semester programme enables you to take classes and join clubs and make friends. A year enables you to really settle into the country and the academic system and to consolidate your learning.

What Is Realistic Academically?

How does the study you wish to undertake abroad fit with your studies at home? Take advice both from your course coordinator at home and the exchange office at your university. Will the courses you wish to study provide you with academic credit? Will your grades abroad be counted in your grade point average (GPA)? Consider taking courses that will broaden your knowledge of the country you are studying in. For example an Australian ecology course may involve research in the field on a tropical island in the Great Barrier Reef.

What Is Financially Possible?

The tuition fees for many study abroad and exchange programmes are negotiated by your home university, but make sure to check this carefully. There may also be opportunities for you to obtain bursaries or scholarships to help you with your travel and living expenses. Check with your study abroad office about this and look at the websites listed at the end of this chapter. In some countries it may be possible for you to continue to receive government subsidies while you are away if you are studying full-time. However, careful financial planning is required. Begin by researching the average price of accommodation and the cost of living and public transport. The website of the university you wish to visit should be able to provide this information, and country-specific information is available from sites listed at the end of this chapter. Also consider trips you would like to take while you are in the country, and budget for this. It could mean that you need to save for a year before you go, or to take out a loan in order to be comfortable and enjoy your time abroad. The best source of information is students who have returned from abroad; again, consult your study abroad office for ways to contact them. There are also many travel blogs being written by students studying abroad, for example http://www.travelblog.org/Bloggers/.

PREPARATION AND LEAVING

Open-mindedness

Research into key success factors for study abroad has underlined the importance of open-mindedness, that is, being open to new ideas (Hadis 2005). There are two ways to think about this. Certainly it is valuable to learn as much as you can about the culture of the place you will visit before you leave; try to meet some international students from that country and ask their advice. However, be ready to change your perceptions when you arrive in the country: what you have read in a guide book may be a bit different in reality. Try to learn and be positive about all the country has to offer rather than judging it because it is different.

Visa and Passport Issues

Check out this area carefully by asking your study abroad office and contacting the consulate or embassy of the country you wish to visit. Be especially careful when travelling in the European Union if you do not hold a European passport. Be aware of consequences of leaving the Union and coming back in. Make sure you can clear customs at each entry point. This can be an issue for travelling between the Republic of Ireland and the UK. Check up and research every stage of your journey.

Accommodation

Accommodation options range from dormitory or student accommodation to home stay, getting your own place or sharing a house. Each university will have an accommodation service. If possible talk to a returning exchange student for suggestions. If you are planning to rent a place on your own, make sure you have all the necessary documentation (for example bank statements, identity documents). If possible download maps of the area you will be staying in, and public transport routes. This will save time and help you settle at the other end.

Banking

Ensure that you can access funds abroad using your bankcard. Talk to your bank about this. It is unwise to travel with large amounts of cash.

Communication

It is vital that you can communicate easily with your study abroad office, your family and your health insurance hotline at any time. Think about how you will do this, and research what phone options will be best for you in the country you are visiting.

Vaccination and Health Issues

Visit your local health centre or a specialized travel medical centre for information on which vaccinations you need. Also consider consulting a specialist health travel advisory service, for example http://www.masta.edu.au.

Health Insurance

You must have travel insurance to cover you for all the time you are away. Check with your student office and the insurer about all aspects of this policy and what you are covered for. Make sure that their 24-hour contact number is in your mobile phone.

Create a Personal Guide Book

Make sure you do research before you go. A good way to do this is to prepare your own guide book or digital equivalent. Include:

- all key contacts for your university, your accommodation, personal emergency numbers such as health insurance, banking, study abroad office;
- flight information;
- translation of key phrases in the language of the country you will visit;
- addresses;
- recipes from home;

- print or photocopy maps and key information about places you wish to visit;
- customs and lifestyle, key dates and festivals;
- contact details for your embassy and groups from your own country, places where you can get food from home and so on.

Cover this and bind it before you go (http://www.isep.org/).

Do an Online Pre-departure Training Course

If it is the first time you will travel abroad by yourself it is recommended that you attend any pre-departure briefing that your university offers. Also have a look at these free online websites:

- http://www.pacific.edu/sis/culture/ – this free interactive programme focuses on understanding and learning about cultural differences.
- http://globalscholar.us/ is a very detailed course sponsored by the US government which covers in detail all the key issues involved in study abroad.

Although aimed mostly at American students travelling abroad, both these courses are offered free on the web and provide extremely valuable advice.

If you are going to a country where you do not speak the language, try to learn a few words. A nice selection is made for you at the following website: http://www.studentsabroad.com/france/infosheet.html.

Saying Goodbye

You need to prepare yourself for leaving family and friends. Consider having a farewell party and make sure you have the email addresses and phone numbers of all your important friends. Make a regular time when you contact family and friends. Skype, web cams, social networking tools like Twitter and Facebook, a mobile phone with appropriate access, can all help you stay in touch.

DURING YOUR STUDY ABROAD

Arrival and Adjustment

My first impression was these huge mountains coming out of the clouds . . .
I became submerged in a sea of mountains. I felt nowhere near home . . .
although I am normally very confident, that first week all I wanted to do was

> sleep and talk to my parents. I wasn't ready to go outside . . . but after a couple of days I slowly crept outside my tiny apartment and discovered the town . . . once I was outside it was OK. (Australian exchange student to France)

As the student in the above quotation found, be prepared to take some time to adjust. Try to give yourself a week before your classes begin just to sleep off the jet-lag and allow yourself to adjust. Get to know the way to school, local shops and places where you can relax.

Study

> There was a lot more group work than I was used to. Students embraced group work and really got into it. (Australian postgraduate exchange student to Holland)

> I was used to having lots of assignments and was surprised to find that everything was assessed in one big exam at the end. (Exchange student studying business in Denmark)

Be flexible and be open-minded. Studying at another institution will present challenges and you will need time to adjust to new ways of working. Find out as much as you can about:

- how you will be assessed: tests, exams or written work;
- who are the key people who will help you and how and when you can contact them;
- where can you find the resources you need.

Differences

A common observation by returning study abroad students from Europe is the importance of group work, and the large weight given to one single final exam.

If you find you have more exams than you are used to, think about how you can set up a systematic revision strategy. If you are faced with group work, read up on how to make group work a positive experience (see Chapter 7 in this book on group work).

Managing your Emotions

Homesickness

> When you are feeling homesick, don't just call home for hours. Read the online newspaper, watch the online news from your country, this helps you stabilise your feelings. (An Australian student studying in Holland)

> Our American professor told us to prepare for a bimonthly attack of culture shock. (Australian student to Japan)

Studying abroad for the first time can be a roller-coaster of emotions. It can be stressful to live and study in a new environment without your usual networks of social support, and you will use all your inner resources to adapt to your new life. It is quite normal to go from feeling very excited about your trip to being quite down about the challenges you may be facing in a new country. Even simple things like unfamiliar weather or food can make you feel down. Other days you will be delighted by the differences! You may well feel very homesick, and you need to give yourself time to adapt. Also prepare for times when homesickness is likely to strike, such as Christmas, and arrange to do something special with friends.

Learn to manage your feelings and stress
It is important to think about strategies you can fall back on if you feel homesick or overwhelmed by the new culture you are studying in. Some suggestions are given below.

> I love cycling so I joined the local cycling club and made so many friends and ended up following the Tour de France! (Australian exchange student to France)

Find ways to stress-proof yourself, for example take regular exercise, join a club or society or find a new hobby. Make sure to get enough sleep and to eat well. Take each day as it comes and keep an open mind.

Meet up with some students from your own country or other internationals to chat. But don't become dependent on doing this as it is very easy to spend all your time with people from home, and thus miss the opportunities to mix with local people.

Relationships

> The hardest thing for me was leaving my family and girlfriend. (Australian exchange student in Europe)

It is quite normal to miss your friends and family very deeply. One thing that can help is planning your communication: for example arrange to call at a particular time each week, and send photos of your daily experience. But beware of spending all your time on Facebook with people back home. Focus on getting all you can from the time you have, meeting new people and sharing these experiences. If you are in a close relationship, perhaps arrange to have your partner meet up with you during a break. However, plan for the fact that you will be very busy as a student in a new country and may not able to do all the travelling and sightseeing they may wish to!

Making friends with local people may not always be easy. Just as in your own country, local students will be busy with their studies and work and will have their own networks. If you are going for just six months it may be hard to break into those networks. Joining clubs and getting involved in sport can be a natural entry point. Many students report making a rich and varied network of friendships among other international students.

Culture

There may be times when you are confused and perhaps upset about the ways things are done in this new culture. These differences will range across all aspects of life – for example, the way people greet and address each other, and the way women and men interact. In France you may be surprised that you kiss friends once or even twice on each cheek. In contrast you may meet a student from the Middle East who has never shaken hands with someone of the opposite sex. At university there may be differences in the way you interact with your teachers. For example teachers may expect students to speak up in class whenever they have an important point to raise; in other cultures the teacher is treated with great respect and students only contribute when invited by the teacher.

The way feedback is given can also be very different. For example an Australian postgraduate student in Holland was surprised by the way feedback was given:

> The Dutch are very frank, they have their own humour. In the thesis defence, nothing was taboo; people butted in and said I don't agree with that, I don't get this. I had done my homework so I knew what to expect but it was still a shock.

By contrast in other countries, for example Japan, teachers may be less likely to give direct feedback:

> The teacher did not want to tell a student she was failing so she told class mates in the other class that the student was having problems so that they would tell her. (Australian exchange student to Japan)

The best way to view these experiences is to try not to take it too personally, but to see it as part of learning the skills you need to participate in this culture. Like learning any skill it will take time and you will make some mistakes, but the result will be that you gain confidence in yourself as someone who can cross cultures and interact with people from different backgrounds.

Heath and Safety

Physical and mental health
Make sure to have a medical and dental check-up and that you are as well as possible before you leave. Be prepared for the stress living abroad may cause you, physically and emotionally. If you have been suffering from depression or other emotional problems, seek expert advice before you leave. If you need any specific medical or other support, check that this is available and how you will access it. Never travel without comprehensive health insurance.

Alcohol and drugs
Alcohol use is often associated with crime and violence. Take great care drinking abroad where you are not familiar with customs and acceptable behaviour. Using drugs abroad can result in the severest punishment. Avoid this at all costs.

Understand the safety issues in the country and city you are visiting
Your government will produce travel guidelines for the country you are visiting. Follow these carefully. Once you are in the country, find out which areas and activities you should steer clear of.

Public transport
Find out if there are routes you should avoid, and if you must travel at night, do so with a friend. Avoid walking out alone at night, as you do not understand the dynamics of the city and areas that are unsafe.

Avoid high-risk activities
Certain activities like bungee jumping, white water rafting, mountain climbing and shark diving adventures can put you into danger. These activities may not be covered by your insurance. If you choose to participate in such activities, make sure that you have adequate medical support and that your insurance plan does cover such high-risk activities.

('Health and safety' section adapted from http://www.studentsabroad.com/.)

RETURNING HOME

Returning home is another roller-coaster of emotion. While you are elated to be home, you may find you experience a kind of re-entry shock. You have changed, but the people back home may not have. They may be less interested than you feel they should be in your experiences. Your experiences are, however, an extremely valuable resource both for other students going abroad and for international students visiting your country. Look out for volunteering activities through your exchange office, or contact international student services to see whether you can be involved in welcoming students to your country. Finally, update your resume with your wonderful new experience!

'INTERNSHIPS: STUDY ABROAD SQUARED'
(Rubin 2009)

Many programmes offer the opportunity to work, either as a volunteer or with a small stipend. It could be as part of your study or as a separate component. In either case, working abroad is beneficial in that it provides you with a really direct way to experience the culture, and also good work experience for your resume. Types of internship can range widely in terms of job activities. You may find yourself doing simple administrative tasks, or sometimes more challenging assignments linked to your profession. In either case the opportunity to understand global culture, whether that be as a volunteer in a school in Africa or as a clerical worker in a firm in Europe, is invaluable. Check which study abroad programmes offer internship opportunities and research as much as you can to find out about the organization it is proposed you work for. For example, will you need an amended visa? Will you be paid? How many hours are you committed to each week?

For further information read 'Overseas internships jumpstart careers' at http://www.nafsa.org/_/File/_/mayjun09_jumpstart.pdf.

Some opportunities for specific professions are now given, but check with your school for more information.

Service Abroad

Engineers
Engineers are increasingly working in global contexts, and those who have taken advantage of the many opportunities to study and do an internship abroad have a head start in the job market. Many universities have engineering faculties that have formal ties with other institutions; find this out from your faculty office. Engineering students also become involved in volunteer work in developing countries and have the skills to make a huge impact in the daily lives of people who may be living without basic

infrastructure such as clean water. Check if your school offers such opportunities, and consult organizations such as Engineers without Borders. See the US website http://www.ewb-usa.org/, and similar organizations in your own country (Bremer 2007).

Medical and nursing students
Medical and nursing students, both undergraduate and postgraduate, have many opportunities either to study abroad or to undertake internships in the field, gaining invaluable experience in both cross-cultural and clinical skills (Ladika 2008; http://www.nafsa.org/_/File/_/novdec08_feature_nursing_2.pdf).

Many medical schools offer clinical rotations abroad, language and cultural immersion, and research. For example the University of Cincinnati offers students the opportunity to take part in 30–40-person brigades in South America, including medical residents as well as students in medicine, nursing and pharmacy (Leggett 2009; http://www.nafsa.org/_/File/_/mayjun09_intmedicine.pdf).

Teachers
It may be possible for you to take part of your teaching practicum abroad, but it is not always an easy option as authorities wish you to be supervised at home. However the opportunities offered for your personal development by spending time in an overseas classroom are immense (Dessoff 2009). Organizations like Educators Abroad organize teaching placements in over 50 countries for students from Canada, the USA and the UK (http://educatorsabroad.org/).

Study Abroad with a Disability

More and more students with a disability are studying abroad. In the USA the National Clearinghouse on Disability and Exchange (NCDE) can give you information and advice about how people with disabilities can participate in international exchange (www.miusa.org/ncde).

CHECKLIST FOR STUDY ABROAD

To make sure you are well prepared for most eventualities, complete the first part of this checklist before you leave, and the last part on arrival.

Before you Leave

Programme
Will I be given credit for the subjects I wish to study?
Can I take course that I am interested in, for example language or culture study?

Money
Have you made a budget?
Have you found out the cost of living? Consider

- food;
- a cup of coffee;
- transport;
- accommodation costs;
- cost of short holidays (travel, accommodation, equipment hire, for example skis);
- mobile phone expenses.

Visas
Are you sure you have the appropriate visa to study? When does it start, when does it expire?
Check when your passport expires and how you can renew it abroad if necessary.
Does this visa permit you to work?
What will happen if you decide to leave the country for a short break?
Make sure that at each point of entry you will be able to clear customs.

Make sure you have phone numbers

- your contact at the place where you will be studying;
- emergency, police, ambulance;

- health insurance company;
- family;
- study abroad office at home;
- your embassy;
- groups from your own country.

Arrival
What time will you arrive?
Does the university have an airport reception service?
What arrangements have you made to get from the airport to your accommodation?
What contingency plan have you put in place if you arrive late, and possibly at night?

Accommodation
Where will you stay the first night?
What type of accommodation do you want?

- homestay;
- own room in shared house;
- shared room;
- dormitory;
- own apartment.

Health insurance
What does it cover?
How can you access it?

Stuff
Can you carry your bag? (that is, is it too heavy to be practical?)
Does your mobile phone have global roaming?
Do you have the appropriate adaptors for your computer?

After you Arrive

Stay in touch
Check all emergency contact numbers.
Does your phone work?
Who can you contact 24/7 if you need to?
Tell your family and the university that you have arrived.

Recheck all transport information.
How long does it take to get to college?
When is the first and last train/bus/tram?
Check your maps.

Study
Find your timetable and course outline.
Where will your classes be held?
Who are your teachers? How and when can you contact them?
What assignments do you have to do? Do you have exams?
When? Where?
Do you have group work? How will the groups be formed?
Where can you find resources to do your assignments?
Where is the library?
Is there any learning support you can access?

Administration
Are there any administrative things you need to do before you start?
Where is the study abroad office?
When is it open?
Can you email requests or should you come in person?

Shopping
Where can you buy food?
Where is the pharmacy?
When are these places open?

Good luck, and have fun!

NOTE

* Many thanks to Timothy Donnet, Kate Hawkins, Hannah Harding, Peta Kennett Wilson, Lorna Rickerts, Casey Stringfellow. These Australian study abroad students have provided valuable qualitative data about the time they spent abroad. This, along with an extensive review of the literature and the authors' own experiences, have informed this chapter.

REFERENCES AND FURTHER READING

Barribal, L., P. Martin and V. MacArthur (2008), 'UK–US exchange in nursing – provocative pradigm or just a safe option?' http://www.butex.ac.uk/?q=node/65. Accessed 11 March 2010.

Bremer, D. (2007), 'Engineering the world', *International Educator*, Nov–Dec, http://www.nafsa.org/_/File/_/engineeringinted_2007.11.pdf. Accessed 11 March 2010.

Dessoff, A. (2009), 'Teaching the world', *International Educator*, May–June, http://www.nafsa.org/_/File/_/mayjun09_teaching.pdf. Accessed 11 March 2010.

Hadis, B. (2005), 'Why are they better students when they come back?' *Frontiers*, **11** www.frontiersjournal.com/Frontiersbackissaug05.htm. Accessed 10 December 2009.

Hofstede, G. (1986), 'Cultural differences in teaching and learning', *International Journal of Intercultural Relations*, **10**, 301–20.

Ladika, S. (2008), 'Nursing goes global', *International Educator*, Nov–Dec, http://www.nafsa.org/_/File/_/novdec08_feature_nursing_2.pdf. Accessed 10 December 2009.

Leggett, K. (2009), 'Teaching medicine without borders', *International Educator*, May–June, http://www.nafsa.org/_/File/_/mayjun09_intmedicine.pdf. Accessed 11 March 2010.

Loveland, E. (2008), 'Student mobility in the European Union', *International Education*, November–December 2008, 22–5.

Mcormack, K., D. Gadd and J. McCarthy (2008), 'Widening participation in study abroad: a case study of the Northern Ireland Business Education Initiative', http://www.butex.ac.uk/?q=node/65. Accessed 11 January 2010.

Norris, E. and J. Gillespie (2008), 'How study abroad shapes global careers', *Journal of Studies in International Education*, **12**, 1–16.

Queensland Government QETI and IEAA (2000), *The Attitudes and Perceptions of Australian Employers towards an Overseas Experience*, Brisbane: QLD Government.

Queensland University of Technology (2004), *Casey and Lorna's Story: 2 Australian Students in Grenoble (DVD)*, Brisbane: QUT.

Rubin, K. (2009), 'Internships jumpstart careers', *International Educator*, May–June, http://www.nafsa.org/_/File/_/mayjun09_jumpstart.pdf. Accessed 10 November 2009.

Tobenkin, D. (2009), 'Legal minds', *International Educator*, Jan–Feb, http://www.nafsa.org/_/File/_/janfeb09_feature_legalminds.pdf. Accessed 10 October 2009.

Useful Websites

For Australia

http://www.axan.com.au/, Australian exchange alumni network, a vibrant site which shares not only stories from Australians who have been abroad on study but also internship information. http://www.idp.com/ provides information about studying in Australia.

For the UK

BUTEX – British Universities Transatlantic Exchange Association, http://www.butex.ac.uk/, promotes mobility between UK and US colleges and universities.

www.britishcouncil-usa.org/index.shtml. This site provides a wide range of information including information for both US students and students from other countries on study in the UK.

UKCISA, UK Council for International Student Affairs, http://www.ukcisa.org.uk/. In particular, provides useful resources for students wishing to study in the UK and professionals working with international students.

UK Student Life, http://www.ukstudentlife.com/. Information about study, work and travel in the UK.

For Canada
www.britishcouncil.org/canada.htm
www.livelearnandsucceed.gc.ca/

For the USA
http://www.isep.org/students/. This is a network of 275 post-secondary institutions in the United States and 38 other countries cooperating to provide affordable international educational experiences for American students and students wishing to go to the USA.

http://educationusa.state.gov. This US government site provides detailed information about studying in the USA.

For Europe in general
EAIE (European Association for International Education), www.eaie.nl/index.asp. This site incorporates a detailed listing of Internet resources of use to both advisers and students.

For Ireland
See http://www.educationireland.ie/ for information about studying in Ireland.

For Germany
See http://ic.daad.de/sydney/ for information about studying in Germany.

For France
See http://www.crous.fr/ for information about living in France.
See http://www.campusfrance.org/ for information about studying in France.

For Sweden
See http://www.si.se/English/ for information about studying in Sweden.

For The Netherlands
See http://www.nuffic.nl/ for information about studying in the Netherlands.

For other countries and working abroad
http://www.bunac.org/, BUNAC has over 40 years of work abroad experience across the globe.

In-depth free online pre-departure training programme can be found at http://globalscholar.us/.

4. Studying in a foreign culture

We see the world not as it is but as we are. (variously attributed)

EXPECTATIONS

When you consider studying abroad, you do your research and you find out as much as you can about the institution you are going to study at, as well as the location. You will have many concerns about how you are going to live, whether it is safe, and may well choose a location because someone you know is there or has already been there. All of this is sensible, but when you travel to a new country, it is not just a physical journey. It is a psychological one as well. You will have expectations of the new culture and deep psychological links to your own norms, values and established behaviour. Living and studying in a different country is not like going on holiday where you are seldom confronted with challenges that require you to adjust to a different way of doing things.

Of course you know this – at least intellectually. However you will often find yourself unprepared for the emotional response to different ways of doing things.

ACTIVITY

You are expecting a friend to visit you. Write a description of your town, city or country. Write about 500 words.

Now read your description and ask yourself the following questions:

- Did you explain how to use public transport?
- Did you describe what is considered polite or rude when meeting people?
- Did you explain where to get food: supermarkets, open markets, restaurants, cafes, and so on?

- Did you explain how much things cost: rent, public transport, fruit and vegetables, eating out, laundry?
- Did you discuss domestic chores, whether or not there is domestic help, what it costs?
- Did you discuss religious norms, where the places of worship are, when services are held, what the attitudes are to different faiths and manners of dress?

It is unlikely that you mentioned all or even any of these things. Why? Because we take them for granted, they are part of our way of life and we don't consider that others may do things differently. Also, we want to paint our home in a good light. But all of these things may impact on your stay in another country – they are the essentials of living, and people in different place do these things differently.

CULTURE SHOCK

The term 'culture shock' has been around for over 50 years (Oberg 1960; Killick 2008, p. 21). One description by Brislin and Yoshida (1994) and Killick (ibid.) explains that when people are exposed to knowledge differences, they can have an intense emotional reaction. You spend a lot of time learning what your own culture considers appropriate knowledge and behaviour, and it is upsetting to discover that other cultures have very differing views concerning appropriate knowledge. You can find yourself at a disadvantage, when you have been advantaged within your own context.

The shock of culture shock really refers to the specific aspect of cultural adjustment that relates to the degree of psychological comfort felt in the new environment. This is difficult to predict in advance.

Furnham (1997: 15–16, cited in Killick 2008: 23) suggests that culture shock may have quite severe psychological and physiological impacts:

Culture shock is seen as a temporary stress reaction where salient psychological and physical rewards are generally uncertain and hence difficult to control or predict. Thus a person is anxious, confused and apparently apathetic until he or she has had time to develop a new set of cognitive constructs to understand and enact the appropriate behaviour. Writers about culture shock have often referred to individuals lacking points of reference, social norms and rules to guide their actions and understand others' behaviour. This is very similar to the attributes studied under the headings of alienation and anomie, which include powerlessness, meaninglessness, normlessness, self and social estrangement, and social isolation . . . Lack of self-confidence, distrust of others and psychosomatic complaints are also common . . . Furthermore people appear to lose their inventiveness and spontaneity and become obsessively concerned with orderliness.

In most cases the symptoms ease with time as you become more used to the new environment.

STUDENT REFLECTIONS

Red brick buildings with sweeping gothic archways; scholarly academics walking down the corridor. Open lawns with casually dressed students sitting in groups, bicycles carelessly leaning against bushes, engaging in stimulating discussion with professors who had cycled to the campus. My mind was going berserk while I sat in the quiet comfort of the back seat of my chauffeur driven Honda City in a mid morning traffic jam in Triplicane, one of the busiest suburbs of Chennai. The contrast could not have been more acute. Triplicane is full of narrow streets, dilapidated buildings, teeming with crowds, street noises, traffic, like any typical Indian city.

Dreams do come true as I realized a few months later. Crossing a few latitudes and longitudes and walking across the Goodwill Bridge on 11th March 2005, I approached the Queensland University of Technology campus, delighted to se the campus buildings overlooking the botanical gardens and the Brisbane river. This was my first day as a full-time overseas MBA student.

I loved the ambience of the campus, the ibises, the casually dressed students congregated at the coffee shops. My dreams had come true!

The 'University for the Real World' soon brought me back to the real world with a jolt. Owing to the usual issues with getting a student visa on time, I missed a week of lectures. As I found to my dismay, the first week had not consisted of 'How are you? Where are you from?' civilities. One-sixth of the 6 week teaching period was over.

Much as I tried to concentrate I could not focus on reading, listening, understanding, remembering. The lectures were hard to sit through in silence, for someone who had been a travelling sales executive for many years. And academic writing was traumatic to say the least. I had a panic attack during my first exam. In the weeks that followed, many a time I would sit on one of the benches on the Goodwill Bridge looking at Mount Coot-tha in the distance and wonder what the hell I had gotten myself into.

Until . . . I decided to do something about it.

After enquiring at the university I found out that they had just the palliative and promptly enrolled for classes on preparing for lectures, writing and listening. You name it – I attended it. But the truth was that even after attending some of these classes I still struggled to receive, understand, analyse and interpret . . . all I did was fret. I attended the same sessions all over again prompting the facilitators to say 'Haven't I seen you somewhere before?'

Finally, like a toddler taking his first real walk it happened. I was more than halfway through the course but my grades shot up and I was seeing distinctions and high distinctions. So after that initial cold shower in an early Brisbane autumn, I was clearly on my way.

> The lecturers who taught in that first teaching period must surely have wondered about my clearly disoriented state but they helped me learn how the system worked and I finished my MBA with a high distinction. I had well and truly found the 'real' world. (quoted with permission of the student)

Here are comments from a student who saw the pictures of a university, one that offered the quiet reflective atmosphere that was not present in his home town. However, what he did not anticipate was that he might have difficulty achieving in the new environment the way he did at home. He found, however, that with perseverance at university and off campus he could be successful.

ADJUSTING TO CULTURAL DIFFERENCE

Adjusting to the differences you confront may not be just about your limited experience of communicating in a different language. So much around you will be different. One strategy to help may be a better understanding of your own tolerance of ambiguity. According to Budner (cited in Erten and Topkaya 2009), ambiguous situations can be of three different types: new situations, complex situations and contradictory situations. When in an unfamiliar environment, all three may apply. You may not be able to distinguish the clues that help you know how to behave; there may be so much going on that you have difficulty understanding what is expected; or you may find the information you are receiving is suggesting that you behave in ways that would be considered inappropriate at home:

> One very simple example was provided by an Australian student. He had married a Japanese woman and spent a while living in Japan. There one of the least expensive ways to eat out was to visit a noodle house. Here people slurped their noodles, making a great deal of noise, as a sign that the noodles were very good. They were indicating appreciation. The Australian understood this but found it almost impossible to do the same. He had been brought up to eat quietly and that making a noise while eating was considered impolite. He explained that it took him nine months to adapt to this accepted Japanese behaviour.

So tolerance for ambiguity, the ability to operate effectively when the situation is ambiguous, can be an importance characteristic in successful adjustment. People with a reasonably high tolerance of ambiguity are likelier to feel comfortable in uncertain conditions. Understanding your own tolerance for ambiguity can assist you to understand your discomfort and put strategies in place that can be of assistance.

ACTIVITY

Below is a way of measuring your tolerance of ambiguity. It is based on a scale developed by Budner in 1962.

Instructions

Please respond to the following statements by indicating the extent to which you agree or disagree with them. Fill in the blanks with the number from the rating scale that best represents your evaluation of the item.

Rating Scale

1   strongly disagree
2   moderately disagree
3   slightly disagree
4   neither agree nor disagree
5   slightly agree
6   moderately agree
7   strongly agree

_____ 1. An expert who doesn't come up with a definite answer probably doesn't know too much.

_____ 2. I would like to live in a foreign country for a while.

_____ 3. There is really no such thing as a problem that can't be solved.

_____ 4. People who fit their lives to a schedule probably miss most of the joy of living.

_____ 5. A good job is one where what is to be done and how it is to be done are always clear.

_____ 6. It is more fun to tackle a complicated problem than to solve a simple one.

_____ 7. In the long run it is possible to get more done by tackling small, simple problems rather than large and complicated ones.

_____ 8. Often the most interesting and stimulating people are those who don't mind being different and original.

_____ 9. What we are used to is always preferable to what is unfamiliar.

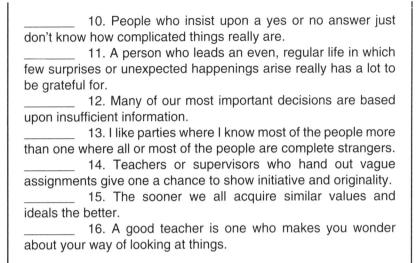

_____ 10. People who insist upon a yes or no answer just don't know how complicated things really are.

_____ 11. A person who leads an even, regular life in which few surprises or unexpected happenings arise really has a lot to be grateful for.

_____ 12. Many of our most important decisions are based upon insufficient information.

_____ 13. I like parties where I know most of the people more than one where all or most of the people are complete strangers.

_____ 14. Teachers or supervisors who hand out vague assignments give one a chance to show initiative and originality.

_____ 15. The sooner we all acquire similar values and ideals the better.

_____ 16. A good teacher is one who makes you wonder about your way of looking at things.

Scoring the Scale

To score the instrument, the even-numbered items must be reversed scored. That is, the 7s become 1s, the 6s become 2s, 5s become 3s and the 4s remain the same. After reversing the even-numbered items, add the scores for all 16 items to get your total score. (Budner 1962 – adapted from people.westminstercollege. edu/.../tolerance_of_ambiguity_scale.doc. April 2010)

Higher Scores Indicate a Greater Intolerance for Ambiguity

So what does this mean for your adjustment? If you have a high intolerance – and the maximum score is 84 – it means that you like to be sure about what is going on around you and therefore will feel the most uncomfortable in a strange learning environment. Learning the new rules and providing yourself with support that makes you feel more secure will be important. If you have a low intolerance level – and the minimum possible is 7 – you may find yourself comfortable in almost every situation. However that doesn't mean you will be successful as you may not pay attention to the detail you need to be successful in the new environment. If you are a research student, your ability to tolerate ambiguity will be crucial. This subject will be further discussed in Chapter 12.

COMPETENCY TIPS FOR SUCCESSFUL ADJUSTMENT

- Understand that you will feel uncomfortable. A good sense of humour often helps, as it will allow you to deal with the frustration and confusion that is bound to occur in an unfamiliar environment.
- Accept that you won't always understand. An ability to tolerate and cope with uncertainty and ambiguity is important. You will often have to take action without all the information you require – or with conflicting information (Lobel 1990). Circumstances change unexpectedly and the behaviours of others may appear unpredictable. Acknowledging that uncertainty and ambiguity exist is the first step. It is important to recognize that multiple perspectives are possible so that you can respond appropriately (Frenkel-Brunswick 1949).
- Language can present a range of problems. You may doubt your fluency and understanding because of the very different accents and vocabulary used. Engage as much as possible with mother tongue speakers so that you get a feel for the language and how it is used.
- Patience and respect are required – by you and the host community. This is important because different cultures have different 'rhythms', they feel different and it takes time to learn what is going on (Ferraro 2002). It is important that you do not benchmark the new culture against your own culture, but try to understand the local reasons for things happening the way they do.
- Develop cultural empathy. Respecting the behaviour and ideas of others requires empathy. Active listening and a non-judgemental approach helps you understand the other person's point of view. This will not always be easy, as empathizing with individuals whose experience and way of viewing the world are significantly different from your own may make you unsure or impatient (Dalglish et al. 2003).
- Be self-confident. A strong sense of yourself and an understanding of your own culture will help. This allows for interaction with people from another culture without fear of losing your own identity.

CROSS-CULTURAL COMMUNICATION

Communicating effectively with others is a challenge in the most normal of circumstances without the added complexity of cultural difference and the issues of second language learning.

Do not expect that it will be easy. Even if you are considered fluent in your own country you may experience many challenges in the new environment. Particularly in English, you will face many different accents: Americans, Canadians, Irish, Australians, Scots, all speak English as their mother tongue but with very different accents. You will also meet up with many people who speak English as a second (or third) language and speak with the accent of their home country. These are challenges that everyone faces when communicating in English.

English has a number of complexities. One English word can have many meanings depending on context, so be aware of the context. An example is as follows:

Trip – can mean 'to fall over something' or 'a journey'.

Be aware of the time it takes to respond in a language that is not familiar. You hear the words in English, translate them into your own language, think of the answer in your own language, and then translate back into English to give an answer. This can take considerable time, so when you want to find out something have the questions prepared in advance so that you can reduce this time. If you are listening to a second-language speaker, be patient: it is not the thinking mechanism that is slow, but the speaking mechanism. Practice, practice, practice. See Chapter 10 for further suggestions.

Assertiveness in sharing opinions is what 'Westerners' are brought up to express. If they have an idea or an opinion, they will express it irrespective of the status of the people they are talking to. Many cultures that are hierarchical find this rude and disconcerting. Their communication is much less direct and opinions or information are provided in a much more indirect way (Holmes and Tangtongtavy 2003).

Be aware of context when you speak to someone who is not familiar with your culture. Much humour is based on shared social experience, for example what was on television, local celebrities. Reference to these will cause confusion. If you don't understand, ask. I know that this is difficult but otherwise you will not understand or, even worse, may understand incorrectly. This is not easy to do as we all communicate within a familiar cultural context and take for granted much of what is 'common knowledge' in our society.

As you will read in more detail in Chapter 10, non-verbal messages play a central role in effective communication. So it is important to understand whether elements of non-verbal language are different from those that you would use in your own society, so as not to inadvertently send the wrong message. Some of the things to look out for include:

- Body language – you way you stand, shrug your shoulders, and so on.
- When, how and where you touch each other, and who you touch. This varies enormously between cultures.
- How, when and where you make eye contact, and with whom. Again this varies between societies, and making eye contact sends very different messages in different cultures.
- How physically close you get to whom, where and when.
- Your relationship with time. How important is punctuality?

All of these things send messages you may be unaware of, and as you will discover they may cause discomfort – to you and others.

Misattribution is the process of (mis)attributing a set of values to observed behaviour. That is, we give a different meaning to behaviour we see than that intended by the person acting. Eye contact is one such behaviour. Not to make eye contact in most Western societies suggests that you are evading something – that you are not being straightforward. However in other cultures direct eye contact with a senior person, or a person of the opposite sex, would be considered disrespectful. The behaviour is the same but the meaning attributed is very different.

Stereotyping, which we all do, provides a mental short-cut to our interpretation of the world – but being a short-cut does not mean that it is accurate. Whenever we meet someone new we have an unwritten set of assumptions which can block effective cross-cultural communication. Think about your stereotypes. What do you expect from the people you are going to study with? How will this impact on your behaviour, and how you view them? Keeping an open mind is difficult, but always check your stereotype against the reality before you act on it. If you are not sure, ask.

GOING HOME

So you have completed your overseas stay and you are on your way home – back to the familiar. But it won't be as familiar as you expect. The same process of cultural adjustment will take place in reverse; the longer you are away, the more obvious the reverse transition will be.

Your home has changed! It is probably you who have changed. You see things in your home environment that you didn't notice before. Your relationships will be different because you have had an experience that others haven't. Suddenly you have to communicate about a context that those around have never experienced. You may not accept things that you did accept before, which can lead to conflict.

For example: A father sends his son to Australia to learn how to run a business – but on his son's return is very reluctant to consider any of the new ideas that the son returns with because they run counter to what has made him successful. The son can become very frustrated as the father sent him away to learn new things – which he appears now to disregard.

Studying abroad is a very important part of any education programme, because it offers a range of challenges that are difficult to find elsewhere. And rising to these challenges enables you to deal more successfully with the challenges that an increasingly global working environment will present. Enjoy the experience, and learn about the challenges and rewards of being a global citizen.

REFERENCES AND FURTHER READING

Brislin, R.W. and T. Yoshida (1994), *Intercultural Communication Training: an Introduction*, London: Sage.

Budner, S. (1962), 'Intolerance of ambiguity as a personal variable', *Journal of Personality*, **30** (1), 29–50.

Dalglish, C., A. Dubrin and P. Miller (2003), *Leadership*, 2nd Asia-Pacific edition, Milton, Queensland: Wiley.

Dalglish, C. and P. Evans (2008), *Teaching in the Global Business Classroom*, Cheltenham, UK and Northampton, MA, USA: Edward Elgar Publishing.

Erten, I.H. and E. Zehir Topkaya (2009), 'Understanding tolerance of ambiguity of EFL learners in reading classes at tertiary level', *Novitas Royal*, **3** (1), 29–44.

Ferraro, G. (2002), *The Cultural Dimension of International Business*, 4th edition, Upper Saddle River, NJ: Prentice Hall.

Frenkel-Brunswick, E. (1949), 'Intolerance of ambiguity as an emotional and perceptual personality variable', *Journal of Personality*, **18**, 108–43.

Furnham, A. (1997), 'The experience of being an international student', in D. MacNamara and R. Harris (eds), *Overseas Students in Higher Education: Issues in Teaching and Learning*, London: Routledge, pp. 14–29.

Holmes, H. and S. Tangtongtavy (2003), *Working with the Thais*, Bangkok: White Lotus Press.

Killick, David (2008), 'Culture shock and cultural adjustment', in C. Dalglish and P. Evans, *Teaching in the Global Business Classroom*, Cheltenham, UK and Northampton, MA, USA: Edward Elgar, pp. 20–36.

Lobel, S. (1990) 'Global leadership competencies: managing a different drum beat', *Human Resource Management*, **29** (1), 39–47.

Oberg, K. (1960), 'Culture shock: adjustment to new cultural environments', *Practical Anthropology*, **7**, 177–82.

www.people.westminstercollege.edu/faculty/mkoerner/00_courses/mtech_616_spr_05/tolerance_of_ambiguity_scale.doc.

5. Benefiting from lectures

Lecturing involves a presentation by a lecturer to a group of students, often large numbers of students. Lectures involve mostly one-way communication – from the lecturer to groups of students that can vary in size from 20 to 2000, with the possibility of questions being raised at designated intervals, and some group work discussions.

Whilst their effectiveness is often discussed, lectures are a part of almost every tertiary course (Smith 1994). The lecture is the standard method for teaching large classes, particularly at undergraduate level.

Lectures are used to transfer information to the student in an efficient, well-structured way. They can also motivate the student to self-study (Barnes and Blevins 2002). In the current climate of easy access to information through the Internet and other electronic sources, value-adding is important. In other words, a lecture takes on a different role in an electronic age where access to information is so easy for the astute student. For a student, there needs to be a serious consideration of what you can do to ensure you get the best value out of a lecture.

For a student to get the most out of the lecture process it is important that you feel supported to integrate socially and academically into the programme you are undertaking, and that the cultural capital brought by you and your fellow students is accepted and valued (Zepke and Leach 2006). The learning environment should be comfortable and non-threatening (Anderson and Moore 1998).

If you are an international student you may experience difficulty adjusting to using English. You may also have difficulty adapting rapidly to many factors in the new environment, of which language is only one (Ryan 2000).

WHEN DOES LECTURING WORK BEST?

Lecturing is only one of a number of teaching and learning strategies that will be used in the classroom. You need to understand the limitations of this method of learning. It is also important that you understand how you learn best, and what factors contribute to your personal learning process. It is also important to recognize that if lecturing is a significant element of the teaching and learning process because of large numbers of students, then you need to develop effective skills to gain the maximum advantage from the experience.

Not every lecturer will stimulate you to think critically and analytically. Lectures cannot be assumed to stimulate high-order thinking (Bligh 1972, cited in Biggs 2003). Also, what happens in lectures is unlikely to inspire or change attitudes. However, there are a number of functions that lectures, well prepared and conducted, can fulfil. These include:

- You can gain information and an overview of the subject (Marshall and Rowland 2006). This can provide common ground for discussion with other students, and serve as a starting point for private study.
- Lectures draw together the main ideas around the topic and provide information about the teacher's personal interpretations. This can offer a unique perspective not to be found in textbooks.
- From lectures you get a preliminary map of difficult reading material and literature that is difficult to find.
- Lectures often provide examples that bring the content to life for you, by seeing how it is applied.
- Lectures adapt a topic in a way that the standard textbook cannot. This can include exploring the relevance to your particular situation, working through issues surrounding the major academic debates in the subject, or exploring in detail the areas that you may find confusing.
- Lectures can direct you to the important areas on which to concentrate before an examination.

Being a student in a large class is not an easy situation to cope with. The tendency to feel that you are an isolated insignificant individual within a large room full of people is heightened when you are a foreign student in that situation. Local students may possibly (but not always) know others, as may some foreign students. Familiarizing yourself with the lecture theatre before the first class and deciding where you want to sit to suit yourself best can be a helpful process. Similarly, arriving early and talking to other students beforehand can be helpful. If you are on your own, understand that there will be many others on their own too, so go up to people and introduce yourself and start a conversation. Many people by nature are shy, so a little effort up front can go a long way to easing the stress of meeting new people.

Give some thought as to how you best function in a lecture theatre situation. Are you a verbal learner or a visual learner? Do you focus best being down at the front of a class or up at the back? Are you easily distracted? If so, where is the best place to sit to minimize distractions? Are you a foreign student or a local student? A foreign student is more likely to have difficulties understanding the lecturer or understanding the examples they use if they reflect the local culture. Do you sit with a local student so that you can ask for clarification on things that you don't understand? In a lecture situation, do you tend to follow the textbook or study guide and write lots of notes? If so, position yourself so that you can spread out a bit without disturbing other students. Have you copied the PowerPoint slides or other lecture material beforehand so that you can write notes on them as the lecturer progresses through the lecture?

Understanding and learning in a large class is not a simple process. There are many styles and processes that different lecturers employ in their work, and as a student it is a good move to watch carefully in the early stages to understand the approach of the individual lecturer. A brief conversation with the lecturer to clarify their approach, and asking how you as a student can best take advantage of the particular lecturer's approach, can often reveal very useful tips.

ISSUES WITH LECTURES

There are a number of issues that need to be considered when using the lecture process, and these issues take on a new significance when you all come from very different cultural backgrounds.

Both the lecturer and you will have expectations and it is unlikely that expectations are shared unless explained by the lecturer. For many lecturers the lecture format is one that is so familiar it is not thought about, and the assumption is often made that you also understand the process. It is easy to understand how this occurs. When you have been doing a particular job or task for a while, you settle into a pattern that is effective for you. Lecturing is very much like that, in that a lecturer develops his/her own style and approach. However, if you are a student attending that lecturer's class for the first time, you may not have encountered this particular approach or style and it can cause some confusion and difficulties. Talking to other students and to the lecturer can help clarify this for you.

Depending on previous education experience, students may view lectures in any number of ways. They may feel they must take down all that is said; that the lecturer's view is the 'truth' not to be questioned but to be internalized. It is not unusual to have questions directly asking for the lecturer's perspective, as this may be the one that appears in assessment. The status of the lecturer differs greatly in different cultures and so the willingness to question or discuss what the lecturer puts forward may vary considerably, and be considered inappropriate by students from many cultures.

How do you feel about challenging the lecturer? How did this process happen in previous educational institutions you have attended? You may not have English as your first language and this without doubt presents a challenge for you and your lecturers. Students' language difficulties are sometimes put down to inappropriate testing, or lowering of standards. This is an unfair judgement as the selection process of the institution should account for this. There is a great difference between doing a test and communicating with native speakers. Local students and lecturers may not understand this. Practice is the key. Remember, it is not easy bringing together many people from many different backgrounds.

Learning a language is much more complex than learning many other skills. Language reflects the history, culture and assumptions of the society in which it is used, and in addition universities use discipline-specific language which is not found in standard language programmes. There may in fact be differences in meaning and assumptions behind words in different countries where people speak the same language, such as England, the USA and Australia. In fact, even if English is your mother tongue you may have difficulty with some of the discipline-specific language. You have only to pick up a book on genetics or astrophysics to appreciate that despite a high level of English language ability, it has not prepared you for the way language is used in such contexts. This raises a further range of issues. Language has the potential to be a significant barrier in a lecture situation, and so it is important that as a student you prepare and position yourself to gain the best benefit from the lecture, whilst acknowledging some of the difficulties due to language issues.

Think about strategies you can use to deal with any language difficulties. Does this institution offer help with language issues? Find out.

Language is a reflection of a culture and can sometimes present interesting challenges. An example of this was a Cambodian student who decided to take 'O' level English in the United Kingdom. Her spoken English was fluent and she did not anticipate any difficulties. However, on completing her comprehension test she approached the tutor puzzled. One of the questions had not made sense to her: this question had referred to a horseshoe. She knew what a horseshoe was – it fits on a horse's hoof. However, what she did not realize was that within English culture, the horseshoe is also a symbol of luck, and the question had dealt with this aspect of the word.

Pronunciation may be an issue. You may never have heard a mother tongue speaker before arriving at university. Also, many lecturers have different accents depending on where they come from. This can make understanding very difficult because whilst you may understand the meaning of the word when seeing it written down, you may not recognize it when spoken. It is important for you to feel comfortable in asking a lecturer for this sort of clarification if you are experiencing difficulties, as this does not reflect poorly on the lecturer or you. It simply acknowledges that how we use words varies in different contexts. And if the language spoken is your second language, the issue is heightened.

Humour has a real contribution to make in a lecture situation as it can help to highlight a point, capture waning attention, or simply be a light moment in between heavy material and content. The use of humour should be handled with care (Beaver 2006). Culture affects what is seen to be humorous; so does context. Humour often relies on 'inside' (local or culturally local) knowledge which may leave you feeling isolated if you do not understand. The joke may even be taken seriously, or significantly misunderstood. One lecturer when discussing different website designs described some of them as 'sexy'. The Australians in the class no doubt understood this terminology and its meaning. However, the following day an international student approached the lecturer genuinely puzzled, saying that she could not understand what the website had to do with procreation. The lecturer now uses more specific language to describe websites! As a student, if humour is being used and you are unsure of its meaning or intent, be comfortable in asking the lecturer for clarification after class.

Telling stories also helps to illustrate a point. Often a lecturer or a fellow student may tell a story to make a point. Often the story will be very local in its content, and not necessarily easily understood by those not from the local area or culture. So, if you have a story to tell, changing the cultural context can be very helpful in ensuring that all your fellow students grasp the meaning and intent of the story.

Lectures may be three hours long. Take food and drink to keep your concentration levels up so that you are not struggling as your concentration level wanes.

Lecturing often involves sustained and unchanging low-level activity on the part of students. Simply sitting and listening lowers concentration. The attention span of a person under these conditions is about 15 minutes. So what can you do to lift your concentration levels? Shift your position in your seat; go through some basic stretch exercises of your legs, lower back, hands, neck; read ahead with your notes; try and think of an example in your mind of something that has been said by the lecturer; apply what is being said to a situation that you are familiar with; write or type some notes on the lecture. There are many and various ways to maintain concentration, and no matter whether the lecturer is sparkling and stimulating or totally boring, you need to work on your levels of alertness.

Lectures, because of the number of students involved, tend to be governed by certain rules and procedures. Rules are established for managing the teaching–learning process. The opportunity for a relationship between you and the lecturer is small and the rules related to submissions, assignments, and so on are likely to be rigid. This may seem unsympathetic. Lecturing, probably more than any other teaching–learning method, offers a very specific level of involvement. The rules are clear, extenuating circumstances are unlikely to be looked upon favourably or even allowed, and when they are, will be managed through an administrative process rather than personally by the lecturer. There are often rules established by the institution for things such as poor attendance and late submission of assignments.

All of this means that as a student you are not necessarily going to feel involved, engaged or valued as an individual. When you are a student from a foreign country, this sense of lack of identity is heightened. However, if you understand the reason for the rules and procedures, you can map out a course of action that allows you to gain the maximum advantage from the lecture situation. Team up with some other students and discuss issues between yourselves; introduce yourself to the lecturer if possible so they are aware of you. If you have tutorials, talk with the tutor about issues and concerns you may have with lectures. Go and seek out student services staff and talk to them. Many universities and colleges have staff whose job it is to support international students. They are aware of the issues facing students and are there to help answer questions and concerns.

ADDRESSING THE ISSUES

Expectations

Being clear about the assumptions and expectations of you as a student is the beginning of understanding the learning environment. If critical analysis, participation and debate are unfamiliar processes to you, then you will benefit from clarifying what is expected of you. Talking to staff or fellow students can help in this regard. Each lecturer has his or her own approach, standards and expectations. Finding out about these early will help you to adjust to the situation and gain benefit from it.

A good lecturer is going to be focused on student outcomes and will seek to help clarify a number of issues at the beginning of a lecture series so that students clearly understand the lecturer's expectations. Here are the things that you, as a student, should expect from lectures:

- That they provide an overall context at the start of a lecture, including important background knowledge students are expected to know so that students can make connections with previous knowledge or experience.

- That they are specific about the structure the lecture is going to take. Lectures can take many forms. They can address several broad areas to ensure that the topic structure is clearly identified. They can be problem-centred, where a problem is described and potential alternative solutions suggested. They can compare different theories or approaches. A lecturer should outline the purpose of the lecture clearly so that the students know what to expect.
- They should indicate the essential reading expected of students and make it clear what they expect of students in reading selectively and appropriately.
- They should understand that students learn best when they feel comfortable, are clear on what is expected of them and feel valued and competent. Classrooms often do not create an atmosphere where students feel safe to learn, and a good lecturer will offer suggestions on how they do their job to aid student learning.
- Good lecturers will explain the importance of a global perspective in learning. They will place emphasis on the expertise in the room and understand that students from different countries and different industries all have something to offer. This creates an atmosphere where specific knowledge is respected and valued.

You make your own contribution to addressing each of these issues. The sense of anonymity for a student can be a problem in large lectures. Setting out to meet other students and to form a small study group or discussion group can assist with overcoming the sense of anonymity. You do not need to feel lonely. Meeting after a lecture to talk about the key points of the lecture can help; asking other students for their view on something that was said in the lecture can help clarify that you have grasped points appropriately; asking another student what they got out of the lecture will help you to understand points that maybe you did not pick up on at the time. Where possible your small group of fellow students should include students from different cultures so that you learn from the different perspectives that come from cultural backgrounds different from your own.

The classroom can be an intimidating place if you have not studied for some time or if you come from a different educational environment and are used to using a different language for your communication. Use the visual aids offered, such as PowerPoint slides or lecture notes. Being familiar with these in advance of a lecture can help you focus your learning without being distracted by your own feelings of strangeness or language difficulty. Making notes in advance can help you clarify points as the lecture progresses. Emailing the lecturer or tutor to clarify a point can help you ensure you are on track.

Language

For many students, language is a significant problem. Converting language to your home tongue is not necessarily a quick and easy process. Added to that are the use of local examples to highlight a point, the use of colloquial language, nuances unique to the home culture, and so on. As a student operating in a second language, the complexity is significant. The barriers to understanding and communication are enormous, and most lecturers do attempt to allow for this in their style and approach. However, this is not always successful – so what can the student do to ease this issue?

- Sit with a local student who clearly understands and is able to shed light on the communication aspects you do not follow.
- Be prepared to ask a question of the lecturer or tutor to clarify something that was said. Understand that asking a question does not reflect a lack of intelligence, only a lack of relevant context.
- Take notes on things you do not understand and seek clarification from the lecturer or a fellow student after the class. You may also seek clarification by reading the relevant material after class to see if it makes sense to you.
- Develop your own notes on acronyms and abbreviations used in lectures. Develop your own glossary of terms used so that you can look them up after the lecture, or ask a fellow student or a staff person.
- Preparation for a lecture cannot be overemphasized. If you have a basic knowledge of the material to be covered in a lecture, you will better understand language issues as you will be able to contextualize them.
- Consider recording the lecture. Many modern universities offer a video or tape recording service of lectures. Enquire whether these services are available, or take your own tape recorder so that you can go back to parts you did not understand and take your time clarifying points.

Engaging with the Lecturer and the Content

Student engagement is difficult in a large class and may not be a priority for the lecturer. Asking questions and openly discussing points can help with engagement if the situation allows for this. If not, sitting with students with whom you are comfortable can help, as can taking notes and engaging in discussion after lectures.

Weimer (2003) noted that students often fear being made to feel foolish by asking a question that is poorly framed or articulated. To overcome this, consider writing the question down first. Also, listen to how other students ask questions and how they frame them so that you learn from your fellow students. You can preface a question by saying that you are from another culture and you seek clarification. A good lecturer will respond accordingly and help you in paraphrasing the question so that the whole class understands it.

Preparation

Preparation is essential for lectures. This point can not be overemphasized. Read the material beforehand, go over the course handout materials such as PowerPoint slides, and make notes on things you are unclear about. Meet with other students before a lecture to discuss what you think are the key points that will emerge in the lecture. Develop your own glossary of terms so that you understand key phrases, terms and concepts.

CHECKLIST FOR GOOD PRACTICE

Have you:

- Read handouts, text, slides, before class?
- Clearly identified the key points that are to come out of the lecture?
- Made a glossary of specialized terms, acronyms, jargon and so on?
- Considered recording the lecture?
- Thought through how you are going to stay focused and concentrating in the lecture?
- Checked that your notes are up to date?
- In your preparation, allowed for the cultural context of the material and thought about how it would apply in your cultural context?
- Considered the cross-cultural issues raised by the material?
- Gained an understanding of the structure and purpose of the lecture so that you can follow it as it develops?
- Gained an awareness of what is the expectation for the particular lecture?
- Identified the areas you do not understand so that you can seek specific information from the lecturer?

REFERENCES AND FURTHER READING

Anderson, M. and D. Moore (1998), 'Classroom globalisation: an investigation of teaching methods to address the phenomenon of students from multiple national cultures in business school classrooms', Working Paper, Monash University, Faculty of Business and Economics.

Barnes, D.L. and D.R. Blevins (2002), 'An anecdotal comparison of three teaching methods used in the presentation of microeconomics', *Educational Research Quarterly*, **27** (4), 41–60.

Beaver, D. (2006), 'Warning, humour can be dangerous', *ABA Banking Journal*, **98** (10), 72.

Biggs, J. (2003), *Teaching for Quality Learning at University*, 2nd edition, Milton Keynes: Society for Research into Higher Education and Open University Press.

Dalglish, C. (2006), 'The international classroom: challenges and strategies in a large business faculty', *International Learning Journal*, **12** (8).

Marshall, L. and F. Rowland (2006), *A Guide to Learning Independently*, 4th Edition, Sydney: Pearson/Longman.

Ryan, J. (2000), *A Guide to Teaching International Students*, Oxford Centre for Staff and Learning Development.

Smith, M. (1994), *Study Secrets*, Mount Waverley, UIC: Dellesta Pty Ltd.

Weimer, M. (2003), 'Focus on learning, transform teaching', *Change*, **35** (5).

Zepke, N. and L. Leach (2006), 'Improving learner outcomes in lifelong education: formal pedagogies in non-formal learning contexts', *International Journal of Lifelong Education*, **25**, (5), 507–18.

6.   The challenges and skills of participation

At my school and at the University I studied my undergraduate degree, we were taught to respect and honor lecturers. It was unacceptable to ask questions of them in class as this showed they had not taught well. We were taught that books are from where you learn. (Postgraduate student in an Australian university)

Effective learning consists of a number of interrelated functions in a learning environment. Being prepared to be an active participant in your own learning will ease the burden of learning, enhance the quality of what you learn, and contribute to you feeling that you are managing your learning process effectively. Participation is about communication and conversation and that creates contacts, interpersonal relationships that lead to friendship. Often university or college life can seem daunting because it is a new environment and in most cases much bigger than your previous learning environment. Through participation you can break that environment down into human dimensions, find friendships, find support networks, and feel more comfortable as you immerse yourself in your learning environment.

Students being actively engaged in classroom activity, supportive of each other and civil in their exchanges is the beginning of effective participation. Class participation is one major vehicle towards achieving quality learning (Petress 2006).

You can become involved through your willingness to ask questions, to answer questions put by the teacher and to engage in discussion activities with other members of the class. These are relatively simple steps, but if you are a shy, retiring person even these simple steps can appear quite daunting.

Research (in the West) shows that learning is an active rather than a passive process.

Most people learn:

- 10% of what they read;
- 20% of what they hear;
- 30% of what they see;
- 50% of what they see and hear;

- 70% of what they talk over with others;
- 80% of what they use and do in real life;
- 95% of what they teach someone else. (Attributed to William Glasser, cited in Biggs 2003: 80.)

It is the 70 per cent figure above that this chapter is focusing on, in terms of reinforcing the message that by talking about what we are learning, we apply it to situations, we reinforce the key aspects and we better understand the theory or principle behind the learning. Assuming there is validity to this summary of learning effectiveness, participation and the opportunity to talk over with others what you are learning does greatly increase the effectiveness of the learning process. Participation in the classroom increases the activity that you are engaged in and extends the learning you do through seeing and hearing and talking it over with others. Other activities such as working in groups and the use of case studies in the classroom extend the possibilities for participation and are covered in detail in following chapters. The lecturer is not the only person with expertise and useful insights.

Most teachers have a genuine interest in the learning and achievements of their students, and encouraging participation is one mechanism for improving the learning potential of the classroom context. Participation as a strategy draws on what we know of effective adult learning. It enables you, the student, to ask questions to identify the relevance of what is being discussed to your particular circumstances. It provides an opportunity to learn about other places, different industries and practices, and individual points of view. It provides an opportunity for knowledge and perspectives to be discussed in a range of different contexts in which the issues may arise. All of these enhance learning effectiveness.

Participation can enhance the relevance of lectures. In large classes, this occurs through tutorials where you are able to interact on a more personal level with other students and the tutor. And it is in the tutorial situation that you are expected to participate and where you can experiment with participation as you learn how to utilize this process.

Participation enables you to check the accuracy of what you have learned and discuss its relevance to your context. It also enables the tutor to assess the level of understanding that you and your fellow students have, and to direct your thoughts to contemporary issues where students from particular countries or industries may have specialized knowledge. In other words, it encourages you as a student to learn from other students and their experiences and situations that are relevant to the topic being discussed. This increases your knowledge as you listen, and as you share your experiences relevant to the topic in hand.

This principle of encouraging you as a student to share your experiences is particularly relevant in postgraduate and MBA classrooms. You arrive as a postgraduate student with a vast range of contemporary knowledge. You are often at the forefront of changes in industries and economies because you have been out there and doing it, as have all your fellow students. You can comment on the impact of changes in the global environment from a practical perspective, providing tangible examples that can be used to discuss the significance of theory. Keeping up to date with the rapid changes in the 'real-world' environment is extremely difficult for academics, but the classroom is filled with students like you who have first-hand knowledge and experience. Often you can provide a significant contribution to discussion around theoretical concepts.

It is very common for students not to realize what they bring to their own learning and to the learning of others. When discussing a particular theory or model you may find yourself thinking about it in a particular context that is relevant to you and your experience. To be able to share that with other students, who come from different backgrounds and different experiences, enriches their understanding and puts the learning into another context that enhances the learning experience for all.

What effective participation also does is enhance the individual student's self-image as they contribute to the accumulated knowledge of the class. If learning is a process of discovering one's personal relationships with people, things and ideas, class participation would appear to be an ideal tool. The classroom is a safe environment where we can try out things that we are not good at and learn more about ourselves without fear of ridicule and rejection.

If you come from a cultural background where the teacher is highly revered and it is seen to be disrespectful to ask questions or comment on what is being taught, then your capacity for active participation is going to be much lower than that of a student who comes from a more open learning environment. For instance, in Australia, university lecturers will often be referred to by their first name, they will expect students to ask questions and they will expect students to challenge things they say. For some students this is a highly challenging situation.

However, if this is not a learning environment you are used to, a quiet word with the lecturer should alert them to the need to assist you to adapt gradually to the situation. They might form a small group discussion and encourage all students to listen to each other. They might give you a question in advance and ask it of you in class, knowing you have had time to think about it in advance. Lecturers generally are responsive to the needs of students. Another action you may like to take is to talk to some fellow students and explain that this is different to what you are used to, and ask them how they handle themselves, what they do, how they cope with an interactive learning environment. The bottom line is that it is important to understand that participation does improve your learning experience, and that you will be better equipped personally and educationally by becoming an active participant in your own learning.

ISSUES CONCERNING PARTICIPATION: AN OVERVIEW

While participation appears to be a very effective learning process, research suggests that participation reduces in classes where there are significant numbers of international and, particularly, non-native English language speakers. Whilst local students appear to be willing to talk publicly, present their point of view and discuss issues, international students appear much more reluctant to do so. This being the case, classroom participation can become a process that separates rather than engages students. So why do international students generally show a reluctance to participate in the classroom?

International students may not have any experience of discussion-based approaches to teaching and learning, so this needs to be handled sensitively (Ryan 2000). Knowing that you are expected to 'participate' in the classroom discussion can cause enormous anxiety for many international students. This lack of experience can mean that you need to understand the purpose of discussion, why it will be beneficial and what exactly is expected of you.

Not speaking the language of instruction fluently can also be a barrier. Participation can be inhibited by fear of embarrassment, of making a mistake, using incorrect English and the resulting loss of face. Even if you wish to participate you may find that you are slow to respond while you think of the right words to use, and find that someone has made their point before you. This can be frustrating.

Sometimes examples given in class are ethno-centric, relating only to the culture, environment and context of the host country. The international student may understand nothing of the example and feel totally incapable of contributing to a discussion on it.

Students can feel that they are wasting others' time by asking questions or expressing an opinion. You may also feel that it is arrogant to put forward your view. This does not mean that you don't have a view, rather that culture and custom makes it difficult for you to express this view in the classroom context.

There are times when the local students do not understand or appreciate the difficulties an international student is encountering in an alien environment, and this can be expressed in a myriad of negative ways that inhibit the international student from wanting to participate. A sensitive lecturer will be responsive to this and manage the expectations appropriately, but sometimes you may need to raise it and seek lecturer assistance.

In some cultures, asking a question of the teacher would imply that the teacher has not explained well, showing a lack of respect for the teacher (Ryan, 2000). This is not the case in most English language-based universities.

ADDRESSING THE ISSUES

As a student many of these issues can seem beyond your control. However, there are steps you can take to minimize the negative aspects of participation and address positively the issues raised in this chapter.

Expectations

Expectations are very important, particularly if you are a student who has had no previous experience of participation. Ask for an explanation about the purpose of seminars and tutorials, or any situation in which you are expected to 'discuss' the information you have been provided with. What sort of participation is appropriate? Can you ask questions? Will the lecturers or tutors ask questions of you? Why are they using this approach? Many students may feel that the teacher's voice is much more important than that of another student, and therefore will not listen and learn from other students' contributions. Seek clarification from the staff person or another student on this.

Understand the 'rules' and expectations. How should you ask questions? When can you or should you ask questions? If there are going to be direct questions of individuals in class, ask for the topics and readings in advance so that you can prepare. Do not feel pressured to respond instantly. If you have to translate the answer from your native tongue into English in your head, say, 'I am translating the question in my head', so that the lecturer and the class are aware of what you are doing, and then respond to the question. It is appropriate to indicate that as English is your second language it takes a little longer to comprehend and respond to a question.

Ask the lecturer or tutor what sort of questions he/she is likely to ask, so that you have a framework in your mind as you read and prepare.

You need to understand that lecturers want to be clear about their assumptions and expectations at the beginning of a course, and that they know this creates a supportive and non-threatening learning environment. It may be difficult for you to ask this question of the lecturer, but you can talk to other students and ask if they would help you to seek clarification at the beginning of a course. Lecturers and tutors are very comfortable doing this, and are likely to do so without you needing to ask.

Whilst participation and debate may be familiar to some students, all students will benefit from understanding what is expected of them. Each lecturer has his or her own approach, standards and expectations. Making this clear to the students greatly assists the learning process and reduces many of the irritations that lecturers experience with students who do not appear to understand. If your lecturer does not do this, here are some thoughts to help clarify.

What does the lecturer mean by participation? Is it just how much you say? What you say? Do you have to say anything? Is participation being measured, and if so, how?

Having a Comfortable Learning Environment

Students learn best when they feel comfortable, are clear on what is expected of them and feel valued and competent. Some classrooms do not create an atmosphere where you feel safe to learn or to share your experiences or perspectives. If you find yourself in a situation like this, talk to other students about how they are finding the learning environment. If they are not having the same experience as you, you can talk about it with them and seek their ideas on how to cope with it. If they do agree, perhaps a number of students can approach the lecturer to talk the issue through. This is definitely not to create a conflict situation, but is to create a conversation about how to enhance the learning environment for everybody.

Understanding the global perspective of our multicultural classrooms is important. Understand that you are one of many going through a similar experience. All are students and whether local or international, many of your experiences are similar. Identify, acknowledge and accept the expertise in the room, and that students from different countries and different industries all have something to offer. Take advantage of this by introducing yourself to other students, asking questions of them and sharing some of your experiences with them. Let others know that some of this is different or difficult for you, and encourage them to identify what they find different or difficult. You will be surprised by how many students, be they local or international, actually share many of the thoughts that you have about the learning situation. This creates an atmosphere where specific knowledge is respected and valued. This enhances self-confidence, a prerequisite for participation.

International students go to Western universities to study because they want to understand their methods, and advance their careers, not because they think that somehow learning from a different culture implies something negative about their own homeland. Similarly for any students who attend a university in another country. Sometimes in a classroom there may be a feeling that one local environment is 'better' than another. This is not intentionally done. It is often implied through use of examples; use of local language; use of local customs, norms and mores; use of local mannerisms and communications. Being sensitive to how this can occur unintentionally is important for a visiting student so that they don't feel isolated or undervalued. Sometimes bringing up a conversation around these issues will be enlightening for everybody, helping them be a little more self-aware and understanding of the nuances of language and cultural difference.

Seeking out and creating opportunities for socialization between you and other students is a significant step in addressing many of these issues. Often issues can be identified and perceptions influenced through simple conversation between students and staff, without the need for confrontation or conflict. It is a truism that most people enjoy meeting other people and accept other people for who and what they are. It is often our social phobia about meeting different people that stops positive interaction occurring.

Sometimes meeting with a small group of fellow students before a lecture can allow a brief conversation to occur about the topic and likely questions or interactions that may arise. This simple process can help you to be more prepared and alert as to what might be expected of you. This has a number of advantages. It gives you time to find the right words. It gives you the opportunity to try an idea out on another student so that the risk of appearing foolish is greatly diminished. It tends also to improve the quality of the participation that you may engage in.

Another thing that you as a student can do is to pair with another student; preferably not a student from your own culture. This pairing comes about through having a conversation with other students, identifying those who you feel comfortable with and asking if they would like to pair with you. Sit in class together, swap notes, talk about issues and concerns, seek advice and confirmation, and so on. This way, when a situation arises about which you are unsure, you can seek clarification. If there is some aspect of participation that is of concern to you, you can seek advice and support in handling the particular situation.

Working in pairs encourages your self-confidence. Pairing can facilitate you meeting each other and benefiting directly from the diversity present. Pairing of people from different industries and different age groups as well as from different cultural backgrounds emphasizes diversity, and if you are to accept the benefits, not just the challenges, of working in diversity, this gives you first-hand experience that may prove invaluable for example when in the workplace you are negotiating with someone from another country.

Language

Many international students do not want to draw attention to themselves. Many experience a culture shock that they did not expect, particularly early in their programme of study. This can undermine their self-confidence and their belief in their ability to be successful in such an unfamiliar environment.

Silence and passivity are seen as virtues in many cultures and it can be difficult to overcome deeply ingrained cultural practices. International students, or any students for whom English is not their first language, when faced with stressful situations such as oral presentations or answering questions in class may feel that they are not adequately prepared to participate with dignity and without loss of face. It is important to understand that in a student setting, loss of face is not an issue of significance and that no one will think less of you. It is well worth remembering that some time ago in America a survey was administered, asking people what their greatest fear was. Being burnt alive was the fourth-greatest fear; speaking in public was their greatest fear. Would the results of such a survey in any other country necessarily be substantially different? Anxiety and awkwardness about presenting in public is common to a vast majority of individuals, so anticipating that you may make a fool of yourself in a classroom presentation is probably exactly what every other student is thinking.

People who speak a second language appreciate how difficult it is to adjust instantly to responding quickly to a question or comment. Acknowledge that it is a challenge for you and that most people understand this. If you can get to feeling self-confident and valued you are much more likely to participate and gain the benefit such participation brings.

Preparation

Preparation is essential for effective participation. You need to know exactly what is expected of you and why your participation is important. You also need to think of the situation in which you find yourself. Are you familiar with the room, the environment, the people? If not, what can you do to help yourself? Go to the lecture room before your first class. Sit in it, move around the room, try sitting in different seats. Where do you think you will be most comfortable? Read the course requirements in advance – what do you not understand? What is confusing? Contact the lecturer for clarification beforehand so you feel better prepared on day one of the first lecture. Go to class early on the first day. Talk to other students (remember this is all new for them too), and find people who you might be comfortable with for the first lecture. Introduce yourself, remember their names, and if the lecturer arrives early, go up and introduce yourself. This can make you feel a little more comfortable.

A LECTURER'S PERSPECTIVE

So far the points made have been from a student perspective. What follows are some best-practice ideas offered to lecturers. The purpose of including this is to help you, as a student, appreciate what a lecturer might be doing in terms of participation, and to recognize the various practices a lecturer might employ. If you understand this and see it happening, it will give you confidence to participate through awareness of what the lecturer is doing and what he/she is expecting. Sometimes putting ourselves in the shoes of the other person helps our understanding and our capacity to cope with different situations.

These are some suggestions that we made to lecturers in a companion book to ensure that students in their classes had the full opportunity to participate and therefore enhance the learning process:

- Include tasks that require participation by all students. Think of ways in which everyone can be active. In a large class this may mean students working in groups before individuals respond to questions. This ensures that although not everyone can address the whole class each time, everyone has been part of the discussion.
- Initially set very structured tasks with clear guidelines. Start with something simple, and as students become more confident with discussion and asking and answering questions, the tasks can become more complex. This helps everyone.

- Encourage international students to ask questions. Talk about cultural difference – the importance of their perspective for everyone. Give positive reinforcement. Students are proud of where they come from – allow them to share this pride. Ask them about relevant examples or experiences from their culture.
- Use a range of different types of participation. Be creative. Ask questions, encourage students to ask questions, use games and quizzes. Any activity that gets students thinking in a meaningful way about the content of what you are teaching will enhance learning.
- Let students use their own words and ways of expressing themselves. Don't correct their English if what they are saying is understandable. If it is difficult to understand, ask them to rephrase it – be supportive and encouraging and encourage your other students to be the same.
- Most people need time to think if you ask them a question. If you are going to ask direct questions during class, let your students know beforehand so that they can prepare.
- Recognize that reversion to their native language is sometimes necessary or a relief mechanism to enable international students to sort out their thoughts.
- Students need to be sure of what is expected of them under the rubric of 'class participation'. This is particularly important if their 'participation' is to be assessed. It must be clear what the criteria for effective participation are. Petress (2006) argues for quantity, quality and dependability:
  - Quantity: It is desirable that all students be given the opportunity to participate by asking questions, offering examples when called for and supplying evidence of personal awareness of concepts relevant to the class discussion.
  - Quality is the appropriateness of the response and participation, avoiding such behaviours as repetitive responses, monopolizing participation, or behaving in such a way as to discourage others.
  - Participation dependability means that both fellow students and teachers can rely on the student to attend class regularly, be attentive, not chat with others in the class and come prepared.

CHECKLIST FOR BEING AN EFFECTIVE PARTICIPANT

As with any other teaching method, preparation is very important. The more you think through how you will participate and what you hope to gain from it, the more effective you will be at handling participation. Effective participation means that you are open to contributing in a range of ways in the classroom, such as asking questions in class, participating in small group discussion, participating in large group discussion, and preparing material before a class if it might help you and others in class.

That participation is not easy goes without saying. Some students are more confident with participation but you will tend to find that the majority of students are cautious and anxious about class participation. Know you are not on your own, and treat participation as part of your learning process. How can you be more effective at participating? What skills do you need to develop to participate effectively?

Have you:

- Clearly identified objectives for the session?
- Identified what you need to feel you are in a safe and supportive atmosphere in which your participation will be non-threatening to you?
- Sought to understand what the expectations for participation are?
- An awareness of your own issues and concerns about participation, and have you prepared as best you can to handle the situation?
- Thought about how you can use participation to enhance your own learning?
- Read the lecture notes beforehand so that you are familiar with the material and aware of what questions may arise in class?
- Thought about how you can meet other students and share experiences with them in the class setting?
- Considered pairing with another student beforehand to help you better handle the expectations and actualities of participation?
- Identified other activities you might undertake that require participation so that you are better prepared for classroom participation? For instance, joining a student body.

For further ideas see Chapter 10 on speaking.

REFERENCES AND FURTHER READING

Anderson, M. and D. Moore (1998), 'Classroom globalisation: an investigation of teaching methods to address the phenomenon of students from multiple national cultures in business school classrooms', Working Paper, Monash University, Faculty of Business and Economics.

Barnes, D.L. and D.R. Blevins (2002), 'An anecdotal comparison of three teaching methods used in the presentation of microeconomics', *Educational Research Quarterly*, **27** (4), 41–60.

Becker, W.E. and M. Watts (2001), 'Teaching economics at the start of the 21st century; still chalk-and-talk,' *American Economic Review*, **91** (2), 446–51.

Biggs, J. (2003), *Teaching for Quality Learning at University*, 2nd edition, Buckingham: Society for Research into Higher Education and Open University Press.

Dalglish, C. (2006) 'The international classroom: challenges and strategies in a large business faculty', *International Learning Journal*, **12** (8).

Dallimore, E.J., J.H. Hertenstein and M.B. Platt (2006), 'Non-voluntary class participation in graduate discussion courses: effects of grading and cold calling', *Journal of Management Education*, **30** (2), 354–77.

Hadjioannou, X. (2007), 'Bringing the background to the foreground: what do classroom environments that support authentic discussions look like?' *American Educational Research Journal*, **44** (2), 370–99.

Harrington, C.F. and T.J. Schibik (2004), 'Methods for maximizing student engagement in the introductory business statistics course: a review', *Journal of American Academy of Business*, **4** (1–2), 360–64.

Levy, L. (2004), 'Most pressing issues in higher education: drawing out the voices', *Phi Kappa Phi Forum*, **84** (4), 56–7.

Petress, K. (2006), 'An operational definition of class participation', *College Student Journal*, **40** (4), 821–3.

Ryan, J. (2000), *A Guide to Teaching International Students*, Oxford: Oxford Centre for Staff and Learning Development.

Weimer, M. (2003), 'Focus on learning, transform teaching', *Change*, **35** (5).

Wentland, D. (2004), 'A guide for determining which teaching methodology to utilize in economics education: trying to improve how economics information is communicated to students', *Education*, **124** (4), 640–48.

Yamane, D. (2006), 'Course preparation assignments: a strategy for creating discussion based courses', *Teaching Sociology*, **34** (3), 236–48.

Zepke, N. and L. Leach (2006), 'Improving learner outcomes in lifelong education: formal pedagogies in non-formal learning contexts', *International Journal of Lifelong Education*, **25** (5), 507–18.

7. Working in groups and teams

> Being forced into group work at university taught me so much about why I never want to work in groups again. (Comment from a graduate student)

The argument often used in universities is that having students learn to work in groups reflects the real world of everyday life in the workplace. However, does it? Is group work and working in teams in a university environment the same as working in teams in the workplace?

Research has long indicated that group interaction is a good way for students to learn (Nastasi and Clemens 1991; Slavin 1991; Johnson 1998). Barber (2003), in discussing non-English speaking students, comments on how teamwork is essential for understanding and emotional comfort. She identifies how teamwork helps students avoid embarrassment, and provides an opportunity to ask questions in a conducive environment which helps them to internalize the topic and relate it to their own situation at home.

From a historical perspective, group work in universities was seen to be an extension of lecturing as a means of imparting knowledge. Many of the aims of group work were to enhance the lecture process. This led to the view that group work only existed to support the proper business of teaching, which was the formal lecture. Stenhouse (1972) and Bligh (1986) promulgated the view that group activity was to teach students to think and to engage with their own and others' learning through the articulation of views.

Group work can be seen as an 'exciting, challenging and dynamic method open to use in a variety of forms and to serve a range of purposes appropriate to different disciplines' (Griffiths 2003). However, the experience of students is often not that as described by Griffiths. Students often see it as a lazy way of teaching, feel forced into a situation they do not understand, lacking the skills to be effective in group settings, and do not feel that lecturers are clear in their expectations of group work and its purpose.

Where do students learn on how to work effectively in groups? From your perspective as a student, group work has a lot to offer, and in fact can be a major component of effective learning, but only if there is clear understanding of expectation and process.

In the context of this discussion, where our focus is on learning in the global classroom, groups are combinations of students formed together to achieve discussion, synthesis, and/or assessment within a learning environment. They may consist of students of varying ages, gender, experiences, cultural backgrounds, levels of commonality of language and levels of expectation within the particular academic environment.

GROUP WORK IN THE WORKPLACE COMPARED TO A UNIVERSITY OR COLLEGE SETTING

Many workplaces do put teams of people together to work on a particular issue or project. Where some collective thinking is required, or cross-departmental involvement is required, teams of staff working in groups can and do provide a useful forum for working something through. And, just as in a university setting, sometimes you are put into a group with some people whom you may not necessarily like or admire. However, there is an existing commonality in that you work for the same organization; you share the culture, goals and aims of the organization; you choose to work there; you either know or are aware of the other individuals; and you are comfortable in the environment, having worked there for some time; and you are being paid for your work.

Group work in a workplace is usually clearly defined in terms of purpose, expectation and outcome, with clearly enunciated time lines. The organization knows what it wants, when it wants it and how it wants it, though it may not know how.

Being familiar with the workplace and the people goes a long way to reducing the stresses of working in a group and towards enhancing the potential outcomes of group work in order to help the group work effectively.

In an academic learning environment, group work has a number of different elements that impact on effective group work. The purpose of forming a group is often to complete some form of learning or assessment. This framework does not imply that all students see it the same way. If you are a student who is aiming to get top grades in every subject, then your focus with group work is a lot different to that of a student who is simply aiming to pass the subject. If the particular subject you are studying is one that fascinates you and forms part of a major component of your degree, then again your focus is a lot different from that of the student who does not enjoy the subject and struggles with the content.

Students often do not get to choose their groups. So cultural, age, gender and focus issues become significant. If culturally you are uncomfortable openly discussing things with a person of the opposite sex, then your learning is impeded. If you are in a group with an older, more experienced person, he/she is likely to lead the conversation and you may feel you have little to offer because of your inexperience. The way groups are formed in a learning environment is significantly different to what may happen in a workplace, and this group-forming process can significantly impede the learning that you get from the group.

The reason a group is formed in a learning environment can also have an impact on effective learning. Is it to enhance your learning by sharing of ideas and concepts? Is it to undertake an assessment item? Is it to present a perspective to the class? Is it to create questions for further discussion? The purpose and expectation of a group work exercise in a work setting is usually immediately apparent.

However it is worth contemplating whether workplaces can also have many competing rivalries and unclear goals and personality issues; and there can be multicultural issues. So university group work, albeit not the same, can be a training ground – and sometimes the only training ground – for future workplace teamwork.

So let us look at different types of group or teamwork and start thinking about them in terms of how, as a student, you can gain full benefit from the experience and enjoy the learning that comes from these processes.

SHORT-TERM GROUP WORK

There are a number of scenarios where group work can be deemed to be an effective methodology for teaching and learning. Within the course of a lecture, it can be appropriate to form small groups for a brief conversation about an issue or a question that will enhance the students' grasp of the material being imparted. This can be a simple question: How would you handle this situation? Or a more complex set of scenarios where different groups tackle different issues around the same theme? For instance, in a marketing subject you may be asked to give examples of 'push' marketing, and other groups to give examples of 'pull' marketing. Or in a strategy class, you may form five groups, each to discuss one of Porter's Five Forces of industry analysis factors.

This process can deepen and extend your knowledge, enhance your capacity to apply the knowledge, and enhance your ability to apply the knowledge to particular scenarios as though you are the decision-maker.

This process reflects the cognitive constructivism approach that says the task of the teacher is not to pass on to students knowledge that the teacher possesses, but to put the students in a situation where they can construct the knowledge for themselves (Gallagher and Reid 1981). This is a common perspective in Western English-speaking universities.

An extension of this can be where groups are formed and allowed significant time to analyse in depth a particular issue or concept. For instance in a discussion on corporate governance you may be in a group that has been asked to discuss a particular concept, and identify examples to share back with the larger class.

In these 'temporary' group formations some of the more critical issues of bonding around an ongoing task and working together to achieve a common goal may not surface, simply because there is a short-term goal. In this situation, being asked simply to form into loose groups around where you sit can be appropriate. As a student, often these forms of group discussion can be fairly easy although factors like dominant talkers or personalities can make it more difficult for the shy to participate. In this situation there is usually not a group leader and you have to be able to speak up to express a view. If you are shy or culturally not used to speaking up, then this informal type of conversation can mean that you don't get to say what you think. A good lecturer will indicate that they want all members to participate and offer some simple steps to ensure that you are involved in the conversation.

If you are in a classroom where you know the lecturer is likely to use this form of learning experience, you can anticipate the sorts of questions the lecturer is likely to ask of a group, and at least feel a little prepared. Without doubt, pre-reading all the material before a class is one definite way to make the process easier for you.

LONG-TERM GROUP WORK

Forming groups to work on assessment items is a different context and introduces more complex issues and considerations for both the students and the lecturer. Lecturers want to help students participate fully in small group situations so that the learning pay-off is fully optimized for you.

The human element of group work is a critical factor that needs to be recognized and acknowledged. Race (2007: 126) explains that sociological research tells us repeatedly that it is human nature not to be involved with people we don't know. We suffer from thinking that we might make a mistake, look silly or be attacked. We will, however, get involved with people we like. This brings us back to one of the questions in the introduction of this chapter. In a work environment we are often interacting with people over a long period of time, so that we become familiar and accepting of others more readily than if we had just met them. This leads to familiarity, understanding and a willingness to work together, knowing and accepting our differences. In a university setting we meet fellow students once a week in a lecture environment which does not encourage personal interaction. Students are asked to form groups usually very early in the semester when they have not had the opportunity to meet others and get a feel for them.

In a multicultural classroom this raises a range of issues to do with effective learning in the global classroom. These issues include:

- cultural norms and more that predetermine how you relate to other people;
- cultural differences of language and relationships;
- frustrations at differing levels of experience and knowledge;
- differing concepts of adult learning and the learning process itself;
- expectations one has of the result they desire.

The point is that the university scenario is not like a work situation, in that at work you may identify a person who you would not choose to socialize with but who you may well respect for his/her work ethic, knowledge or skill. Therefore you may be quite comfortable working with him/her in a group because you realize that each of you has a contribution to make. In the university scenario you are often forced into a group without preliminaries, and should there be a clash of personality, approach or philosophy you, as a student, do not have the time to allocate to developing a meaningful working relationship or understanding of the other personalities in the group. Group work at university is about squeezing time in around many other time demands to work singularly on a project. This highlights the need to lower barriers quickly with strangers, whilst identifying, acknowledging and respecting different viewpoints, all while focusing on a particular context to do with learning new knowledge and information.

The following discussion on group work is designed to offer tips and ideas that can be beneficial for the student. For much of the material that follows, we want to acknowledge the work of Phil Race, whose many offerings on the learning process are a major contribution to understanding groups and teams in the university setting (Race 2007).

GROUP SIZE

Group size offers varying opportunities and problems that need to be considered. Pairs are limited to short-term functions, can create imbalance of contribution, but can enable a weaker student to learn from a stronger student. Threes provide an easily constructed group with a balancing effect built in for disputes. Free-loading (where a student allows other students to do the bulk of the work) is limited and it is functional for students to arrange to meet and work together. Fours offer opportunity for delegation and collaboration, bring out the differing strengths of students, and allow for diversity in ideas and process. Fives allow for a casting vote as well as depth of work for the same reason as fours. Free-loading potential is increased with size and this can become apparent in groups of five. Beyond five in a group, issues of coordination are increased dramatically, as is the potential for free-loaders. Consideration needs to be given to the task and the function of the group to ensure that a larger group is going to achieve desirable learning outcomes.

As a student, consider the different implications of your group size and be aware of these, so that when you are placed in a group you can operate within your comfort zone, understanding the broader ramifications of the group.

GROUP FORMATION

Formation of groups can be handled in many differing ways. Some examples were mentioned earlier in the chapter. Some other group formation techniques may include friendship groups based on students naturally self-selecting. Geographical groups can take two forms. The first is the students' geographical positioning in the room, so that it is easy to converse in classroom discussion. Another form in the global classroom is to consider the geographical nature of the various cultures represented in the classroom and to allow like-minded cultural groups to form. Conversely, deliberately to create intercultural interaction to allow students to draw on the diversity of their geographical background can enhance their learning and understanding. As a student, you can influence this process by who you sit near in class, and by having a conversation with the lecturer about what sort of group you would like to work with.

Another group formation technique can be alphabetical (first letter in the name or last letter in the name) or age groupings depending on the make-up of the class. There are also any number of random techniques for group formation, such as astrological groupings, performance-based groups and skill-based groups. As a student you are at the whim of the lecturer in terms of how they decide to form groups. However, a conversation with a lecturer telling him/her what you think will help your learning process can often create a good awareness.

The critical aspect of group formation is to take account of the task to be set, the time frame available and the purpose of using group techniques. Understanding the basic interactions of groups helps to ensure that a group process enhances the learning experience for you, as well as allowing you to perform to your potential capability.

SOME ISSUES AND IDEAS TO CONSIDER

A clear understanding that group work can help you make sense of the learning and apply it practically to various scenarios, and the benefit of interaction and sharing of knowledge, skills and experiences, are good reasons to participate. For full-time students, group work is easier to organize, arrange and manage. For part-time students, it is problematic. Group work adds a significant pressure point in the busy schedule of a worker attempting part-time studies. Asking a lecturer to be aware of this aspect could encourage group interaction during breaks and within the normal class time as well as in external time, which can ease some of the negativity automatically attached to the concept of group work.

The role of a student in group work can vary enormously depending on the make-up of the group, the size of the group, the function of the group, and the personalities within the group. Understanding these variables can lead to a meaningful discussion on group work practice within a group. In cases where a group is going to meet numerous times, it can be very healthy to have a discussion at the first meeting about issues such as: Is there to be a leader? If so, what is their function? Coordinate? Delegate? First amongst equals? Adjudicating? Facilitating? That leads to a conversation on the role of group members and how a group effectively allocates tasks, and performance indicators. In group work there are many followers, and understanding that followership is in fact an art in itself and effective followership is equally as important as effective leadership can help clarify people's attitudes towards their function within a group.

A discussion in the group about what can go wrong with group work can be enlightening and beneficial in assisting you to become more aware of the pitfalls and take corrective action where necessary. This is as much your responsibility as that of the other group members. Some of the issues in a group can include:

- performance indicators;
- equally distributed workloads;
- punctuality;
- commitment to process;

- preparation and contribution to a meeting;
- disruptive behaviours such as domination and passive resistance.

Openly discussing these early on can help a group bond more quickly, feel comfortable with each other more readily, and focus more clearly on the task at hand, knowing that they are informed about how they will work together. An open discussion on these aspects can also assist you all in acknowledging your individual behaviour and attitudes, and reflecting on these within the context of a group process. Openly discussing a range of these points in the first meeting can assist the group in developing a strong and focused energy. Writing down what you have agreed can avoid disagreement later in the process.

Margerison and McCann (1995) developed a team management system to help assist teams to have a better understanding of the strengths and weaknesses of the team and its members. They identified eight core work functions that underpin effective teamwork. It might be interesting for you to consider these functions and decide which one you are comfortable with, and then ask the other team members for their opinions. The outcome can be an easy method of identifying the potential of your group to work effectively, as well as the potential problems you might encounter where one or more of the functions is not covered by a team member. The eight functions are as follows:

- Advising: gathering and reporting information.
- Innovating: creating and experimenting with ideas.
- Promoting: exploring and presenting opportunities.
- Developing: assessing and testing the applicability of new approaches.
- Organizing: establishing and implementing ways of making things work.
- Producing: concluding and delivering outputs.
- Inspecting: controlling and auditing the working systems.
- Maintaining: upholding and safeguarding standards and processes.
- Linking: coordinating and integrating the work of others.

In a global classroom, awareness of cultural issues and sensitivity towards these is imperative. An ethnocentric ('my way of looking at the world is the best way') approach severely limits the willingness of others to contribute. Acknowledging that in some cultures students will wait until spoken to before they speak, or that learning is about the experts sharing their knowledge and not about the students sharing their experiences and views, or that some cultures encourage debate and free thinking, are all factors that students should consider in their groups. There are many different ways to achieve a goal, and the fact that one person's way might be different to another's does not mean that one is less relevant or realistic. A process-driven person has as much to contribute to a learning experience as does a results-driven person. Understanding and acknowledging these variations can lead to insights and learning beyond the subject matter of the particular course or subject.

An open discussion of possible sources of conflicts within group work scenarios is a useful exercise in creating awareness as well as tools for handling potential conflict situations. What conflicts can occur? How can you identify the root cause of the conflict? How can you establish ownership of the conflict and therefore identify possible avenues for resolution? How can you ensure conflict scenarios do not destroy a project or a process? How can you be creative in the use of conflict to enhance the outcomes of the process or the learning through the process? Often the open discussion around these questions will have students identifying how to handle various conflict scenarios, and the roles to be played within a group either to avoid conflict or to ensure appropriate handling of the conflict situation. This is a critical element in learning to use group processes and should not therefore be 'delegated' to a referee (usually a lecturer or tutor).

SUMMARY

Group work is a very positive learning technique in a university setting, but it needs to be managed effectively and you need to be aware of the processes that can lead to complications as well as those that enable you to avoid the pitfalls. The message in this chapter is to be aware of the different factors influencing group work and to carefully and thoughtfully to think about how you will manage yourself in that setting.

The key points of this chapter are:

- Group work is a teaching tool in its own right that can contribute uniquely to the learning experience.
- Allow for the cultural differences in your group.
- Acknowledge that it is human nature to not be involved with people we do not know.
- Try and create 'get to know you' opportunities.
- Understand that different group sizes create different dynamics, and know how to work with these.
- Encourage your group to discuss roles and functions and expectations up front.

- Openly discuss problems with group work, and positive approaches to overcome the problems.

REFERENCES

Barber, P.D. (2003), 'Teaching non-English speaking students', *Adult Learning*, **14** (1), 29.

Bligh, D. (ed.) (1986), *Teaching Thinking by Discusssion*, Guildford: SRHE and NFER Nelson.

Gallagher, J.M. and D.K. Reid (1981), *The Learning Theory of Piaget and Inhelder*, Monterey, CA: Brooks/Cole Publishing.

Griffiths, S. (2003), 'Teaching and learning in small groups', in H. Fry, S. Ketteridge and S. Marshall (eds), *A Handbook for Teaching and Learning in Higher Education. Enhancing Academic Practice* (2nd edn), London: Kogan Page.

Johnson, D.W. (1998), 'Cooperative learning returns to college', *Change*, July–Aug, 26–36.

Margerison, C. and D. McCann (1995), *Team Management*, London: Management Books 2000.

Nastasi, B.K. and D.H. Clements (1991), 'Research on cooperative learning: implications for practice', *School Psychology Review*, **20** (1), 14–19.

Race, P. (2007), *The Lecturer's Toolkit. A Practical Guide to Assessment, Learning and Teaching*, New York: Routledge.

Slavin, R.E. (1991), 'Synthesis of research on cooperative learning', *Educational Leadership*, **48** (5), 71–82.

Stenhouse, L. (1972), 'Teaching through small group discussion: formality, rules and authority', *Cambridge Journal of Education*, **2** (1), 18–24.

8.   The case method: 'learning by doing'*

Students learn more effectively when they are involved in the learning process (Bonwell and Eison 1991; Sivan et al. 2000). Learning can take on many forms and the case method has developed a solid reputation as a meaningful contributor to the learning processes of students. Almost invariably, as a student you will come across a case study in your university experience. The case method is a problem-based teaching method which is based on a 'real' and authentic situation.

It is a century ago that Harvard Business School implemented the case study method for teaching business. Over that century, the methodology, experience and practice of case study learning has been refined and the core principles laid down at Harvard University. Cases are now used around the world covering all kinds of disciplines across both undergraduate and postgraduate programmes. By the mid-1990s Harvard alone had a library consisting of over 30 000 cases, with 5000 of these functioning in practice as a resource for universities all over the world (Kjellen et al. 1994).

Case study learning is a fully participative model of learning. It is based on the Socratic method which has been a fundamental learning approach. This involves the students discussing and developing their responses to problems posed. It is not a learning process where you can sit back and not contribute. You are actively involved and contribute at various levels which will be discussed.

The basic tenet of case study learning is that the student does not learn by memorising endless lists of facts, models and theorems, but needs to learn to question, to develop the habit of logical reasoning when faced with a problem. It strongly supports the notion of critical analysis and objective reasoning. It is not the 'correct' answer that is being looked for, but the process by which a person came to their answer. As a student you have the opportunity to apply your learning to a 'real' situation. This can be a lot of fun as well as challenging your ability to apply your knowledge. Whilst case method does not tend to teach 'theory', it assures that theoretical knowledge will be applied to solve the problem presented.

A case is a description of an actual situation, commonly involving a decision, a challenge, an opportunity, a problem or an issue faced by a person or persons in an organization. The case allows you to step figuratively into the position of a particular decision-maker. A case, therefore, can be a media article describing some particular event or happening; it can be a prepared document detailing a happening; or it can be created to bring out certain information and processes. The essence is that a case is field-based to allow the blending of theory and practice.

Cases enable you to learn by doing. By placing yourself in the shoes of the decision-maker, you enhance your preparation to become totally professional in your field of work.

Some of the key features and the core principles that underpin case methodology help us to understand more clearly the case method and its unique contribution to learning. These include:

- The teacher is not a teacher per se but a facilitator of learning. He/she is the catalyst in the exchange between you, the student, and the learning process.
- Case studies are based on 'real life' situations. They should reflect the actuality of an event or set of circumstances so that you are operating in 'real time', not simply learning a theoretical framework.
- Case studies are based on decision-making and problem-solving. Their inherent purpose is to encourage you to solve problems and make decisions as though you are actually involved in the situation.
- Good case studies do not encourage you to identify one right answer. The purpose behind a case study is to encourage you to analyse the situation and to draw your own conclusion based on your learning, knowledge and experience. It is the journey to the answer that is critical, not the answer itself.
- The basis of case study learning is critical analysis. As a student you bring your knowledge, experience and learning to the table and it is your level of interaction with the case that facilitates effective learning. Case study learning is not a passive learning process. You are involved.

To further our understanding of the case study method, Mauffette-Leenders et al. (2001) identify an inventory of skills developed by the case method:

1. Analytical skills. The case method enables you to develop qualitative and quantitative frameworks to analyse business situations, including problem identification skills, data handling skills and critical thinking skills. You are forced to reason clearly and logically in sifting carefully through the data available. This may be an unfamiliar activity for you and may require an explanation from the lecturer of what is involved.

2. Decision-making skills. The case method pushes students, on the basis of their analytical work, to assess what can be done and to make decisions. You learn to generate different alternatives, to select decision criteria, to evaluate alternatives, to choose the best one, to formulate congruent action and implementation plans. This requires a level of confidence that many students may not have. However, a good lecturer will encourage you to value your expertise and perspective, and to draw on others who have knowledge that may be useful in this particular context.

3. Application skills. Cases provide an opportunity for you to practice using the tools, techniques and theories that have been learnt.

4. Oral communication skills. The case method provides ample opportunity not only to listen to colleagues but also to express views. Thus, a whole set of speaking, listening and debating skills are developed. In this exchange of ideas and arguments, you learn to think on your feet, and to consider others' viewpoints as well as to defend your own position. There are particular issues here for students for whom English is not their first language. You will need to prepare in advance and think through your unique contribution and think about what you would be able to contribute to any decision-making.

5. Time management skills. Under the heavy pressure of case preparation and juggling of various other responsibilities, students are forced to schedule educational activities carefully and manage time effectively. This is a good skill to learn for later work life.

6. Interpersonal or social skills. The case method, through small group and large group discussion, promotes learning how to deal with your fellow students. This learning includes conflict resolution skills and practicing the art of compromise. Because so much of future work life will involve committees, task forces, boards or project teams, learning to work effectively in a group will help you differentiate yourself from others.

7. Creative skills. Because no two business situations are quite the same, the case method encourages looking for and finding solutions geared to the unique circumstances of each case. This method invites you to use your imagination in problem-solving, as there are normally multiple solutions to each case. So it encourages you to think broadly and widely and to draw on lots of ideas as opposed to seeking only one right approach.

8. Written communication skills. Through regular and effective note-taking, case reports and case exams, you learn the skills associated with effective writing. Emphasis on writing skills varies depending on the programme the student is enrolled in, but does takes on a high priority in many programmes as it is a key factor of success in many professions.

A summative comment on the case method comes from Professor Katherine Merseth of Harvard Education School, when she says that right from the start the case method 'was grounded in the obligation of professional education to prepare practitioners for uncertain practice' (Merseth 1996). Given the difficulties faced by international students, the case study method, if managed carefully, would appear to have great potential to help develop the skills all students need, and reflect the multinational and multicultural context within which we all work.

WHY DO STUDENTS LIKE THE CASE METHOD?

An argument for the case study method suggests that repetition of practice leads to good practitioners. The quantity of exposure to excerpts of reality results in growing professional skills (Christensen et al. 1991). In other words, the more you try and deal with a real-life situation, the better you become at making sound decisions and analysing information effectively. Feedback from students indicates that whilst it may take a little experience to get used to case studies, once they are familiar with the process they really enjoy the learning process and the fact that it allows them to explore ideas and come up with their own solutions.

A little educational theory helps us understand the role a case study can play in the overall learning experience of an individual. Bloom's (1965) Taxonomy of Cognitive Learning classifies a broad range of learning outcomes into six learning objective categories:

- Knowledge. State terms, specify facts, definitions, categories, ways of doing things. (No evidence of understanding is required. The learner needs only to 'boomerang' back the information given).
- Comprehension. Change the information to a more meaningful parallel form, paraphrase, interpret, infer, imply, extrapolate when told to do so (lowest level of understanding).
- Application. Apply understandings to solve new problems in new situations when no directions or methods of solution are specified.
- Analysis. Identify components, how they are related and arranged; distinguish fact from fiction.
- Synthesis. Produce a new combination not clearly evident before (requires originality or creativity).
- Evaluation. Form criteria, make judgements, detect fallacies, evaluate, decide.

The case method has the capacity to address all six levels of Bloom's Taxonomy. Depending on the level required by the lecturers, they can manage the case study process to the required level of learning. In other words, the case method allows for addressing all levels of Bloom's Taxonomy in a planned and coherent manner. This brings out the best in students as they apply their knowledge and experience to the situation.

WHAT IS EXPECTED OF THE STUDENT?

Case study learning requires students to take an active role in their learning; to respect the ethical framework of respect, trust and openness with their peers (particularly regarding diversity and confidentiality); and to be fully committed to ongoing learning. Chapter 6 provides guidelines on encouraging participation that apply equally to case study activities.

LEARNING THROUGH CASE STUDIES

The educational challenge of a case has three major dimensions to it. As a student, take time to understand these three dimensions as this will allow you to move quickly into being very effective in working with cases:

1. The analytical dimension raises the question of: What is the reader's task with respect to the key decision or issue in the case? Being able to sift through the data supplied, determine the crux of the issue and determine potential outcomes is an analytical process based on the parameters of the case at hand. Cases can have varying degrees of difficulty in terms of the information supplied, requiring varying degrees of analytical skill in determining outcomes.
2. The conceptual dimension is concerned with what theories, models and concepts are useful in understanding a particular case. In some cases these may be identified; in others there may be readings associated with the case that indicate the relevant theories; and in other cases you have to draw from your body of accumulated knowledge to determine what theories are applicable.
3. The presentation dimension revolves around the question: What is really important and relevant information here and what is still missing? A case with a low degree of difficulty is short, well organized, contains all the information, offers little extraneous information and is conveyed in a single simple format. A more complex case in terms

of presentation is the opposite of the above points. It is long, disorganized, missing relevant information and includes much extraneous information, and is presented in a multiple style format.

THE CASE STUDY PROCESS

Case study learning involves three stages of interaction and activity. The first is individual preparation, which is the most important in terms of maximizing the potential benefits to you, the student. Familiarizing yourself with the case and identifying what theoretical material is relevant is paramount to successful learning with cases. You need to be encouraged to come up with the right analysis, solution and implementation, just as if this was a real-life situation in which you had been placed. Effective individual preparation sets the foundation for the following stages.

The second stage is small group discussion which is the link between individual preparation and large group discussion. There are a number of reasons why small group discussion is important:

- Teaching others. To understand a case fully a student needs to be able to discuss it fully so that others understand where they are coming from with their suggested outcomes. This can be a safe environment to test your ideas and thinking, as you are with a small group of fellow students, usually with whom you have some rapport.
- Encouraging individual preparation. Small group discussion is one way of ensuring everybody prepares. Peer group pressure is quite severe in a small group when one member has not completed the work expected of him/her. Be sure you have done the pre-reading and that you are ready for a conversation about the case and the course work it relates to.
- Speak about every case. In a small group all members have the opportunity to express themselves, which is not always the case in a large group.
- Develop communication skills. Small group participation enables students to practice listening, talking, expressing and persuasion skills that enhance their overall capacity as communicators.
- Recognize good ideas. Comparing one's ideas to another's, recognizing that another's ideas are better than your own, and improving ideas through interaction with others, are all outcomes of small group work.

- Foster teamwork. Every work environment requires the ability to work with teams of people. This is a fundamental skill that small group work encourages and enhances.
- Build confidence. In a small group it is easier to argue a view, debate alternate views, and express yourself with confidence.
- Build relationships. Small group discussion can be tough and demanding, but many meaningful relationships evolve from the camaraderie that develops through open, trusting communication.

The third stage is large group discussion. This is where the total quality and quantity of the debate and discussion should emerge. It is in this forum that the depth of a case may emerge from the interactive input of all the participants following their individual and small group preparation. Whilst you may have a concern or fear about expressing yourself in a large group discussion, there are a number of reasons why you should be prepared to participate:

- Learn by doing. Knowing that you may be called upon to make a comment sharpens individual preparation and enhances your learning process.
- Respond as requested. Knowing you may be called upon to participate keeps you focused on the discussion and helps to keep your thoughts ordered.
- Teach others. An individual's insights and views will be different from those of others in the class, and all students have a responsibility to share their knowledge and experience to allow others to learn from them.
- Practice public speaking. In many workplaces you will be required to speak in front of others. Large group participation develops the ability to speak in public with confidence.
- Be included. Your sense of belonging and participation is enhanced as you participate in discussion and debate.
- Test ideas. The security of a classroom environment allows you to test your own ideas and thinking against those of others around you. Unwillingness to share thoughts can be seen to reflect a lack of preparation.
- Get good grades. In many case study courses, class participation is an assessable item that influences the final grades. If you are sitting there trying to avoid involvement, in fact your learning receptors are closed off, and the depth of the learning experience will pass you by and this will be reflected in your grades.

HOW TO PARTICIPATE EFFECTIVELY

Individual preparation for a case study is critical in achieving the learning outcomes that case studies offer. A lecturer can facilitate good individual preparation, but it is the preparation that you undertake that enhances your experience. Here are some tips.

Not knowing the industry or the business can seem daunting, but the standard approach to a case study is for you to put yourself in the position of a key player in the case study. This immersion into the role allows you to become familiar with the material within a contextual framework. This approach also ensures you 'own' the problem and do not simply play the role of spectator or observer.

In preparation for a case study you are required to go beyond simply reading the case. You have to anticipate the problems, play out the scenarios for handling the issues and consider the implications beyond the case. In other words become involved in the case as an active participant taking a problem-solving approach to the issues. The opportunity to prepare in advance can provide international students with the confidence to participate.

Mauffette-Leenders et al. (2001) give us the short-cycle preparation process of how to read a case study to ensure effectiveness. This process should take no more than 15 minutes and consists of:

- Step 1 – Read the opening and the closing paragraphs. That is, get a quick picture of the case.
- Step 2 – Who? What? Why? When? How? What are the critical points?
- Step 3 – A quick look at the case exhibits. What is relevant in these?
- Step 4 – A quick review of case subtitles. Is there anything here that stands out?
- Step 5 – Skim the case body. Get the feel for the case and the writing style.
- Step 6 – Read the assignment questions and reflect. What do I need to focus on?

The long-cycle preparation process is composed of both a detailed reading of the case and commencing the case-solving process. The long-cycle process consists of:

- Part 1 – Read the case.
- Part 2 – Apply the case-solving process

- ○ Define the issues. What are the key points in this case?
- ○ Analyse the case data. What are the data telling me?
- ○ Generate alternatives. Brainstorm ideas on how to address the critical issues.
- ○ Select decision criteria. How am I going to make an informed decision on potential actions?
- ○ Analyse and evaluate alternatives. Apply the decision-making criteria to the alternatives you have generated.
- ○ Select your preferred alternative. Out of this exercise, what alternative makes most sense?
- ○ Develop an action and implementation plan. Put it all together in a proposed way forward.

Effective preparation is essential in that the preparation for a case study has to take its place within the busy world in which you as a student operate. Understanding this is more important if you are an international student in that you have to take into account the cultural differences in your environment.

The following tips can help you immeasurably:

- Do not read the case over and over without a road map of exactly what you are looking for.
- Read and prepare at a time in the day when your personal effectiveness is high.
- Block uninterrupted periods of time.
- Follow the principle that scheduled activities take precedence over unscheduled ones.
- Read and prepare during times when you can combine this activity with others, such as eating, or riding on the bus or train.
- Set a time limit for yourself and stick to it.
- There is no need to do all the preparation all at once. Allow time for reflection.
- Draw on fellow students to discuss and reflect on the case. Different perspectives can be invaluable in identifying issues and alternate courses of action.

ENHANCING YOUR PARTICIPATION

The benefit of the case study is often derived from the type and nature of discussion that takes place between all students. Each student brings his/her own perspective to the discussion based on his/her cultural background, experiences, education and knowledge. The interactive process of the group enhances the learning process and encourages deeper understanding and comprehension of the principles the case study is designed to bring out.

The normal case discussion covers five phases:

1.   the start;
2.   the issues;
3.   the analysis;
4.   the alternatives;
5.   the action and implementation plan.

These phases parallel the case-solving model recommended for individual preparation. This consistency will help your learning.

In *Education for Judgment* (Christensen et al. 1991), Christensen makes an extremely important point that bears consideration:

> Teaching and learning are inseparable parts of a single continuum . . . of recip-
> rocal giving and receiving. In discussion pedagogy students share the teaching
> task with the instructor and one another. All teach and all learn.

The key focus of the instructor's role is to facilitate the discussion and to provide opportunities for you to maximize your learning. This can be directive or non-directive but it is based on bringing out learning opportunities for the participants (of which the instructor is one). The key role of participants is to learn through listening, talking and reflecting. The '4Ps' of involvement are the minimum requirement that should be front of mind as you approach case study discussion:

●   Preparation.
●   Presence.
●   Promptness.
●   Participation.

However, to gain and contribute the most, participation must reflect a total commitment to the process. You have to be willing to share your analysis, to subject your ideas to open debate, to take risks and to critique others' positions in a positive manner. For many, this can seem a daunting task. In some cultures, participation in an educational setting is not encouraged and is in fact deemed to be disrespectful. For some, our natural tendency is to be shy and quiet in group situations, and this raises issues of how we can participate effectively. These can be significant barriers to overcome, but you are encouraged to bring such issues to the attention of the instructor in order to find a comfortable path that allows you to contribute within the bounds of the case study methodology.

Effective preparation in group discussion includes using preparation notes to guide input; organizing remarks so that you add to the flow of discussion; and timing remarks to offer maximum contribution to the group. This can take practice and you may stumble early on, but if you persevere, you will find your confidence will grow with every opportunity.

OVERCOMING PARTICIPATION PROBLEMS

No matter what the reason may be for why we do not enjoy participating, there are some helpful hints that can assist you to overcome issues. There are further suggestions in Chapter 6:

- Good preparation is essential. If you feel comfortable with the material you will find it easier to participate.
- Work at adopting an assertive attitude that allows you to feel you have something to offer.
- Seek support from the lecturer. Perhaps the lecturer can allow you to go first to overcome anxiety about participating.
- Whilst culturally this can be difficult for some, make eye contact with people you know and don't look at the whole room. This will ease the sense of anxiety.
- Narrow your visual focus to one or two people so that you feel you are talking to friends.
- Sit near the front of the class so that psychologically you can reduce the size of the room.
- Identify other students who are reticent to participate and link up with them up by them challenging each other to see who can make significant contributions each week. Make it a form of contest to help encourage yourself (and others).
- Make a point of raising your hand at least once a week to offer a contribution.
- Be comfortable seeking the help and support of your lecturer or instructor. They are there to assist your learning.

Large group discussion is an essential part of any classroom process, but particularly so in case study learning. Developing the skill of becoming a meaningful contributor is a learnt task that takes effort and concentration. However, the benefit of learning this skill will stay with you in all walks of life once you have completed your studies. Taking time in a supportive environment to experiment with learning to be an effective contributor will enhance your quality of enjoyment and participation throughout your life. As the facilitator of this process, the lecturer can offer much to your learning beyond just subject content.

There is more about presentations in Chapter 10.

CASE PRESENTATIONS

Case presentations in class can take various forms depending on the preference of the lecturer, the size of the class, the time available and the nature of the case. In terms of effective presentations there are a number of key elements and requirements to take into account:

- Organize the presentation.
- Prepare well.
- Use memory props.
- Keep it simple.
- Use quality visual aids.
- Rehearse.
- Anticipate audience reaction.

In some cases, the lecturer may invite students to provide a critique of a presentation as a means of enhancing awareness of what makes up a good presentation. This can be a very constructive way of helping you to reflect on how you perform under similar circumstances. Giving feedback in these circumstances can be very useful and meaningful if a few rules are followed:

- Be constructive in giving clear, honest and objective comments. Present the good points first and do it in a descriptive manner that allows those being critiqued to understand the points clearly.
- Limit observations to a few important aspects of the presentation – don't try and cover all the minute detail.
- Distinguish between content and process observations. There is the subject matter – what we talk about; and the subject manner – how we talk about it. Distinguish between these in feedback and observations.
- Encourage vicarious learning by considering your own style and modus operandi when presenting. By reflecting on the work of others, we can often learn significantly about ourselves.

CASE REPORTS

Often students will be required to submit a case report or case notes as well as make a formal presentation. These can be used for assessment purposes or simply to gauge the degree of student preparation. Again, there are a few key elements that increase the effectiveness of a case report:

- Be very clear on addressing what is required.
- Review the evaluation criteria.
- Plan the report carefully.
- Write as a manager.
- Check your work.
- Make the most of it: use the experience to practice and improve written communication skills.

There is more about written communication in Chapter 9.

CASE EXAMINATIONS

These can take various forms including a take-home exam or in-class exam, either open- or closed-book. It may be a case previously discussed in class or a new case altogether. With a case handed out ahead of time, the preparation is essentially as that for a case report. Here are a few tips:

- Try to anticipate what type of questions will be asked and what analyses could be required.
- Review cases that may have similarities to this one.
- Make detailed notes of answers to anticipated questions, and organize the notes.
- If prepared well, the exam is a process of organizing your ideas and conveying them effectively.

With an exam based on a case that is handed out in the exam room, the preparation is obviously different and the mindset in the exam is different:

- Manage time wisely.
- If feeling overwhelmed, determine a structured process based on the six steps of the short-cycle process discussed previously.
- Think about how to present the analysis before starting to write.

No matter what style of case exam, there are a range of suggestions that are useful for you to be aware of:

- Find out and meet the lecturer's expectations.
- Plan time according to the marks allocated for each question.
- Focus energy on the content and on writing points clearly and simply.
- Resist the temptation to digress, and stay focused on exactly what is required.
- Support recommendations quantitatively.
- If required, make sure you hand in all exhibits and calculations.
- Use examples of real-life situations. This helps to show that you understand the concepts and theories.
- Be consistent with arguments and assumptions.

There is more about being successful in examinations in Chapter 11.

MANAGING THE LEARNING PROCESS

Case study learning is about developing critical thinking and critical analysis skills. The benefit of case study learning is that it is based on cases from the real world and you are asked to involve yourself as though a participant. This simulation provides hands-on learning and enhances your capacity to cope with and understand life as it really happens. In the work environment we are constantly confronted with dilemmas, problems and situations that require critical analysis and thinking before we can determine an appropriate action. Developing an understanding and a familiarity with the case study method of learning will enhance your capabilities in work environments.

CHECKLIST FOR GOOD PRACTICE

Sometimes a case can be introduced by the lecturer either giving a brief synopsis or asking various students to share briefly with the class the key features of the case. This ensures that all the students have prepared, as the lecturer invites random individuals to comment. This sets the scene for detailed class discussion in either small groups or large groups depending on the teaching plan of the lecturer. An overall framework for the case discussion would include:

- define the key issues and concerns;
- analyse the data;
- determine alternative courses of action;
- decide on a criteria to narrow down the alternatives;
- select the preferred alternatives; and then
- determine a detailed action and implementation plan.

Depending on the case, this structure may vary, but the essence of it is to help students focus on the process of their case discussion. Understanding this process is a significant benefit to you as a student as you approach a case study learning process.

The cultural factors of a multicultural classroom become apparent in the participatory patterns of students. It is imperative to the learning process that all students participate in case discussion, and you should approach the process with confidence that it is OK to participate within a generally supportive environment.

Choosing cases that reflect the cultural background of the class can be significant. Too often it is all too easy to choose cases from the lecturers' country, as they are familiar with the story. However, the rich tapestry of global cases enriches the learning experience as well as reflecting the global nature of business today. As a student, it can be important to understand the cultural differences of how problems are handled. What is seen to be an issue in one cultural context may seem irrelevant in another. Understanding this enhances your capabilities.

CONCLUSION

The case method is a highly beneficial method for student learning and offers many advantages to you. In a multicultural classroom the case method allows for intercultural awareness of practices and takes the student into other ways of thinking about problems and issues. When you immerse yourself in the role of a decision-maker, you are opening yourself to new learning and new understandings that you will not get by more conventional learning practices. The key to the case study method of learning is preparation. This cannot be emphasized too strongly. The more you put into preparing before a class, the better you will feel about what you are learning and about participating in the learning experience. Being comfortable that your own life experiences are worthwhile and that your knowledge and experience brings value to a group discussion is important.

NOTE

* The authors want to acknowledge the seminal works of Louise Mauffette-Leenders, James Erskine and Michiel Leenders in the field of case study learning and teaching (Mauffette-Leenders et al. 2001).

REFERENCES AND FURTHER READING

Bloom, J.S. (1965), *The Process of Learning*, Cambridge, MA: Harvard University Press.

Bonwell, C.C. and J.A. Eison (1991), Active Learning: Creating Excitement in the Classroom, *ASHE-ERIC Higher Education report No. 1*, George Washington University, School of Education and Human Development, Washington, DC.

Christensen, C.R., D. Garvin and A. Sweet (eds) (1991), *Education for Judgment*, Boston, MA: Harvard Business School Press.

Erskine, J.A., M.R. Leenders and L.A. Mauffette-Leenders (1998), *Teaching with Cases*, Ontario: Ivey Publishing.

Kjellen, B., K. Lundberg and Y. Myrman (1994), *Casemetodik. En handbook om att undervisa och att skriva*, Stockholm: Grundutbildningsradets skriftserie nr 14.

Mauffette-Leenders, L.A., J.A. Erskine and M.R. Leenders (2001), *Learning with Cases*, Ontario: Ivey Publishing.

Merseth, K.K. (1996), 'Cases and case methods in teacher education', in J. Sikula, T.J. Buttery and E. Guyton (eds), *Handbook of Research on Teacher Education*, 2nd edition, New York: Macmillan, pp. 75–92.

Myrman, Y. (2001), *The Case Method. Fundamental Principles and New Trends*, Stockholm University, Sweden: Swedish Case Method Centre.

Sivan, A., R. Wong Leung, C. Woon and D. Kember (2000), 'An implementation of active learning and its effect on the quality of student learning innovations', *Education and Training International*, **37** (4), 381–9.

9. Communication: writing in the global classroom*

> An essay of 5000 words . . . I asked myself where are all those words going to come from? (Lisa, cited in Lawson et al. 2004)

Writing is the key skill you will need to develop to be successful in your study. Like Lisa in the quotation above, you may feel overwhelmed by what you have to write. It's not always easy in the beginning, especially if you are writing in a second language. However it is important to remember that it is a skill you can and will learn. Learning to write well in your area will be of great value in the workplace, and giving examples of writing tasks that you have completed in another country looks great on your resume.

This chapter will be organized around some frequently asked questions about writing at university, and it will present some strategies to help you write successfully. At the end of the chapter there are resources to help you develop your writing, including a complete reflective essay written by an MBA student.

WHAT WILL I HAVE TO WRITE?

As you can see from the following example questions, there is a broad range of writing tasks that you may be asked to complete.

Case analysis:

> Your team will gather information about an 'Outstanding' team . . . You will describe the team and then provide your team's analysis on why the team is 'outstanding' class. Then, you will produce a 4–6 page (double-spaced) report due at the end of the course. (Assessment from Managing Teams in the Workplace, University of South Carolina Columbia)

Literature review:

> Students are required to select from a list of consumer behaviour problems currently being experienced by real organizations and conduct a review of

the relevant marketing literature. The purpose of the assessment is for students to analyse and synthesize information from theoretical and real-world sources as preparation for the consumer behaviour project which is due later in the semester. (Assessment from Marketing course, Queensland University of Technology)

Essay:

Each module is assessed by an individual essay assignment and an end of module degree examination. (Assessment from University of Glasgow Business and Management: level 1)

Some of the most common types of academic writing tasks are now given:

- Essay.
- Literature review.
- Report.
- Case analysis (see Chapter 8).
- Online discussion posting.
- Research proposal.
- Thesis.
- Reflection.
- Professional documents.

The Essay

This is a common form of written assessment – the aim is for you to read widely and come to an opinion based on the reading you have done (the evidence). Your lecturer will use the essay to see if you have understood the key ideas in the course and that you are able to do some research and think critically. Most importantly the essay needs you to organize your ideas to give an answer that flows and is logical. Use the structure in Figure 9.1.

Literature Review

This is similar in structure to an essay. You may be asked to do it on its own or as a part of a larger document, for example a proposal or thesis. The aim of the literature review is to understand better a research problem or issue by exploring and critically analysing journal articles and books (the literature). It is not just a list of everything on the topic: it categorizes the literature (for example into themes) and it addresses a particular research question. The

Introduction (roughly 10% of word count)

An introduction typically:

- Makes clear the context of the topic.
- Specifies the major themes or issues.
- Gives the writer's argument; also referred to as 'thesis statement'.
- Outlines the sequence of main ideas the writer will follow.

Body

The body of an essay typically consists of a series of connected paragraphs which follow the outline presented in the introduction. Each paragraph has:

- A central idea (also known as 'topic sentence').
- An expansion or explanation of the idea.
- Evidence to support this idea (examples, data, expert opinion).
- Clear links to previous/following paragraphs.

Conclusion (10–15% of word count)

A conclusion typically:

- Briefly summarizes the ideas and evidence presented in the body.
- Restates/refers back to the central argument.
- Gives a concluding statement.

Figure 9.1   Essay structure

literature review will often identify a gap or area that needs further research. As you read the literature, look for common themes and ways to organize your review. For example, it could be organized from general to specific, in chronological order or around a theme such as the type of research methodology used.

ACTIVITY

Introduction

Look at the introduction from the essay provided at the end of the chapter. Notice how the author achieves a good flow of ideas moving from general opening statement to the specifics of his argument and the plan for the essay.

The Body of the Essay

Now look at the body paragraph of this essay. Notice the topic sentences and evidence to support and expand on this idea. How does the writer link to the previous and following paragraphs?

The Conclusion

In the conclusion, which sentences summarize the ideas and evidence presented in the body? Does the author restate/refer back to the central argument? Does the writer give a concluding statement?

The Report

The report is another popular way to assess your writing, especially in business, science and engineering. The purpose of a report is to communicate information, for example the findings of an analysis (in contrast to an essay that develops an opinion or argument). It usually has numbered sections and headings (an essay usually does not have headings). Check your course outline for the exact details required by your school. A report usually includes the following sections:

- Title page.
- Executive summary or abstract (this gives an overview of the whole report).
- Table of contents.
- Introduction.
- Body (may include methods and materials, analysis, results, discussion).

- Conclusion.
- Recommendations.
- Appendices.
- References.

Case Analysis

This is a common form of assessment, especially in business. You are required to examine a situation in business in the light of the literature and theories in that area. For more information please see Chapter 8.

Online Discussion

You may be asked to post your thoughts on a particular issue onto a website and then to respond to the comments of other students. Take care to understand fully what is expected of you. This is not online chat! While the style of writing can be a little less formal than the style in the documents mentioned above, you will usually be expected to back up your thoughts with evidence and references, and use an appropriate professional tone.

Research Proposal

This document is usually only required at a postgraduate level of study. It provides an overview of your research idea, including an introduction and a statement of the research problem and the research question you will address. Further information is given in Chapter 12.

Thesis

This is the most extensive document you will be asked to write at university, and comes at the end of your course of studies if you have undertaken an honours degree, a masters by research degree or a doctorate. For detailed information see Chapter 12. In Europe the word 'thesis' may be used to describe a large report that you write based on a research project or internship.

Reflection, for example Reflective Journal

In a reflection you will need to write about your own experience in the light of the material you have been learning about in your course. For example:

Describe a problem which occurred when you were working in a team. Analyse and discuss the problem using the theories and ideas you have learned in this course.

With this kind of question you will need to write both in a formal academic style when discussing theory, but also in a more personal way when you are recounting your experience. The last part of the example essay at the end of this chapter provides an example of the style you could use in a reflection.

Professional Documents

In many subjects you will be required to write the type of documents that you will need in your future profession, for example a business plan in a business degree, or a clinical plan in a nursing degree. You will be given clear guidelines on how to do this. Note that you may need to include academic references; this will probably not be required in the workplace.

HOW WILL MY WORK BE MARKED?

Most universities will use a criteria sheet and will give you a grade based on your performance in the following areas:

- Content: this is your understanding of the subject area.
- Research: how broadly and deeply you have read.
- Analysis: how well you select, interpret and organize the key ideas.
- Structure: logical presentation with introduction and conclusion.
- Presentation: correct format, layout, grammar and referencing.

Let's take a look at these points in more detail.

Content

To include appropriate content, the first step is to make sure that you have understood the question and what you are being asked to do. Pay special attention to directive words: for example 'summarize' means to describe key information about an issue, but 'discuss' means to consider and analyse all sides of an issue. What type of document are you being asked to write? For example, is it an essay or a report? Make sure to read all course documents carefully, especially your course outline, your lecture notes and any suggested readings. Do not hesitate to talk to your tutor or lecturer, either in person or by email, to get clarification about the task or the subject.

Research

You will be expected to read widely: books, journal articles and appropriate online documents. For an average undergraduate essay you should read at least ten books, journals or documents. These should be recently published (for example in the past five years) and they should be from reliable sources (check with your tutor or librarian for examples). Typically journal papers should come from 'peer-reviewed' journals, that is, journals which only publish papers which have been carefully read and accepted by other researchers in this field. Most university libraries subscribe to extensive databases that will give you access to a huge range of journals and other documents. Make sure to attend any workshops your library runs on how to use its online resources. Learn which databases are recommended for your subject area.

Analysis

One of the most challenging parts of academic study and writing is learning to analyse the issues and the literature in your subject area. Critical analysis is highly prized and will help you to obtain the best grades, especially in the later years of your degree or at a postgraduate level. It is the key skill that you need to develop your argument.

In an analysis you give your views based on theory and evidence, critically considering a range of different facts and opinions. You will often need to understand theory and apply this to your question. In an essay your analysis will typically be found in the introduction and conclusion, and at strategic points in the essay as you draw attention to your position on the question. In a research report your analysis will typically be found in the discussion as you interpret your findings. In a literature review your analysis will be seen in the way you organize and show your understanding of the literature. In a case study or business report you may need to analyse the strengths and weaknesses of a particular business.

Structure

This is the way you organize your answer. Your writing should be logical and typically starts with a broad opening paragraph which establishes the context and then narrows to specific sets of points in each paragraph, concluding by summarizing key issues and returning to the broader issues in your paper.

Presentation

Your writing should be word-processed, correctly referenced and contain no spelling or grammar mistakes. It should be laid out accurately in line with the guidelines given by your school (for example, submission details, font size, spacing, margins).

WHAT IS AN ARGUMENT?

This is a key idea. Most academic writing will require you to analyse the issues and come to your own opinion about a particular issue based on what you have you read and researched. This is your argument or thesis. Important things to note about this are:

- the need to base this argument on evidence (your careful and critical reading, for example of a range of academic books and journal articles);
- to be logical in how you present the argument;
- to use a neutral and academic style, for example 'This paper will argue that' rather than 'I believe that'.

Think about the following question:

Critically evaluate and discuss the following statement:
'In the twenty-first century, all students should study abroad for at least one semester'.

The key words that show you how to approach this question are 'critically evaluate' (to consider a number of views and decide the strengths and weaknesses of each) and 'discuss' (to explore in words all sides of a question). To answer this question well you would need to develop your thoughts about the value of study abroad and present these thoughts in a logical way considering both:

- the advantages, for example the opportunity to learn a new language and culture; and
- the disadvantages of study abroad, for example expense and disruption to study.

You would use evidence from your reading and research (for example the improved job prospects or personal growth of students who have studied abroad) to develop an argument supporting the statement or disagreeing with it.

WHAT IS DESCRIPTIVE WRITING? WHAT IS CRITICAL ANALYSIS?

Many written tasks will require you to do both descriptive writing and critical analysis. For example in a report you may have to describe results and then discuss these results.

Descriptive writing gives information using description or summary. In a question that requires you to give a description, question words would thus be:

- Describe.
- Summarize.
- Outline.

Analytical writing goes beyond description and seeks to highlight key aspects of the information, to explain and understand it. In a question that requires you to give an analysis, key words would thus be:

- Discuss.
- Evaluate.
- Compare/contrast.
- Explain.
- Analyse.

Look at the differences between description and analysis in these two texts. Which is descriptive, which uses critical analysis?

Text A
In any year 1 per cent of college students in the USA are studying abroad. Of these, over 80 per cent are white and over 66 per cent are female. Most are middle or upper class and most go to Western Europe for a short period of time.

Text B
If study abroad programmes are to make a significant impact on the future education of US citizens and to meet the challenges of living in a competitive challenging global environment, such programmes must reach out into the community and provide the means for students from all ethnic and economic backgrounds, not just wealthy white female students, to study abroad. The elitist nature of programmes needs to change so that all students have the opportunity to study abroad for longer periods of time and not just in Western Europe.

In Text A the author simply describes the fact and figures about study abroad in the USA. In Text B the author critically analyses these trends, discussing their impact and arguing for the need for change. (Information from Kean and Hamilton 2008.)

WILL I LOSE MARKS IF MY ENGLISH IS INCORRECT?

This is something you will need to check with your lecturer, but generally some marks are given to English expression. However, even if only a few marks are allocated to expression, grammatical and spelling mistakes give a bad impression of the quality of your overall work. If English is your second language, ask a native speaker to proofread your work. Check whether your university can help in this area with language and learning advice.

HOW CAN I IMPROVE MY WRITING?

> With assignments I would write draft after draft and get my friends and family to review them and give me some feedback and I would take on board their constructive criticism and improve my writing. (Chinese Australian business and law student)

Getting feedback from others can be a very useful tool to improving your writing, as this student found. However be careful if sharing with another student doing exactly the same essay. Your work is expected to be independent and original. See the comments on plagiarism later in this chapter, and in Chapter 11 on assessment.

Above all, to improve your writing you need to take control of the writing process and make sure you leave yourself enough time to edit your work. You are unlikely to receive a good mark if you hand in something which is essentially a first draft. Understanding the writing process, particularly time management, is vital to your success.

Give yourself enough time and get started with reading and planning as soon as you can. Roughly three to four weeks is needed for an average 2000–3000-word assignment.

Learning Advice Services

Consult your university website for information about workshops and special lectures on writing.

SUGGESTED TIME PLAN FOR AN ESSAY

Week 1

Plan your time, make a reading and writing plan. Analyse the question, do preliminary reading, outline an answer, develop a structure.

Week 2

Keep reading and researching. Write a first draft including a rough working introduction (don't worry if this is not very good; it gives you a starting point).

Weeks 3 and 4

Further reading, editing, rewriting, final editing (check marking criteria sheet, spelling, grammar and flow, and ask yourself: 'Have I answered the question?') Submit!

Learn from Reading

- When you read textbooks and journal articles notice how these experienced writers explain ideas and develop their argument. Take note of how they introduce other authors – for example: 'Blake (2007) argues that . . .'.
- Pay special attention to the introduction, conclusion and opening sentences.
- Notice how paragraphs are structured, how the main idea of the paragraph is introduced in the topic sentence and how the writer links from one paragraph to the next.

Look for books on academic writing in your library and on university websites (some examples are given at the end of this chapter).

HOW CAN I IMPROVE MY READING?

A first step in improving in your reading is to manage your reading time:

- Establish a reading timetable: for example, make an hour available to read before the lecture.
- Manage your concentration levels: read new material when you are fresh; when you have less energy, make summaries, copy diagrams and make notes.
- Use active reading strategies:
  - Read with a question in mind.
  - Read the abstract or chapter summary as a guide to how to read.
  - Scan for the information you need.
  - Use headings to guide your reading.

Make Notes with a Purpose

Get the facts if you need these (for example for an exam or a description) but also look for the author's argument, how they summarize their key points and what evidence they use to support their argument. This will help your critical analysis. Note sections you need to read again in detail. If one section is very difficult to understand, try reading another textbook (use the index or table of contents to find the same topic).

HOW CAN I REFERENCE MY WORK?

At university it is necessary to reference accurately any words or information you have taken or cited from another source (for example from a book, website, newspaper, DVD).

You need to reference when you use a direct quote (the exact words from another author) and also indirect quotes, when you give a summary of someone else's material, paraphrase someone else's ideas, copy some information or use a picture, table or some statistics which are not your own.

Accurate referencing must have two parts: the reference to the author or source immediately before, or after, you have given the information, and the full details of the reference in your reference list at the end of your paper. Use the style your school requires, for example the American Psychological Association (APA) style is common in psychology, sociology and business. Law commonly uses footnotes. The essay at the end of this chapter is referenced in a version of APA style. Check for the most up-to-date version of the style your school requires.

WHAT IS PLAGIARISM?

Plagiarism is when you use other people's work without a reference. This may be a mistake, the result of not understanding the rules of referencing or a careless error. It can also be quite deliberate. With access to the Internet it is easy for students to cut and paste large amounts of text into their own work. This is easily detected through the software most universities now use to check students' work. If deliberate plagiarism is proved, it can mean you fail the subject and in some cases lose your place at university. To avoid plagiarism, reference everything you have taken from another source.

For further information see Chapter 11 on assessment.

HOW CAN I WRITE IN MY OWN WORDS AND PARAPHRASE?

In addition to referencing carefully all the authors you use in your work, it is also important to put ideas in your own words and integrate the words and ideas of authors into your own work. You must clearly show how a quotation from another author or a fact relates to your argument. This requires you to develop your academic vocabulary and your writing skills. To do this, make notes about what you read in your own words, taking care to note the source of all material your read.

A number of the books listed at the end of this chapter will help you to improve your ability to include the work of others in your writing.

COMMON PROBLEMS WITH WRITING

Flow

A common problem for students learning to write is that their writing doesn't flow. This can be the result of poor organization of material; for example your body paragraphs do not follow the order you said you would use in the introduction, or the ideas in the paragraphs don't develop in a logical, ordered way.

Another problem is that the ideas do not 'stick together' and read as one integrated piece. In Scandinavian countries students are taught to think of a red line or thread (*røde tråd*) that runs through their work, connecting their main ideas. Good flow in your writing comes from clear thinking that enables you to develop your argument and to build the case for your point of view from your introduction to the topic sentence in each paragraph and to your conclusion. You make your ideas flow by linking them together with words that link and signpost what you are saying.

For example:

- to introduce a contrasting idea: while, however, but, although.
- to add more strength to your point of view: in addition, another, moreover.
- use of pronouns that refer back to your argument, for example: this/ that, these/those; 'These differences are clearly seen in the example of . . .'.

Carefully repeating the key words in your argument is another way to hold your writing together. When you are reading a textbook or journal article notice how the writer helps you to understand the flow of their ideas using these techniques.

Paragraphs Too Short or Not Well Organized

Your paragraphs are the building blocks of your essay:

- They need to contain at least three sentences.
- A paragraph should contain one main idea which is expressed in the topic sentence.
- This idea must be developed sufficiently with examples and evidence. There is a concluding statement and then a link to the next paragraph.
- The paragraph as a whole should be coherent and contain only information that is relevant to the topic.

Style

> This introduction looks too easy, in my country we like to make it more complicated to make the reader interested and challenged. (Student from the Middle East)

Writing in English at university, you should use a clear style and structure and your work should be easy to follow, not complicated! In fact a clear, simple style is of great value in both academic and professional writing.

However there is a difference between spoken academic English and written. Consider the following example:

Text A – Written academic English:
'A number of inconsistencies were revealed in recent research.'
Text B – Spoken academic English:
'In some work I did recently I found a whole lot of confusing things.'

Text A uses the passive voice ('were revealed' and formal vocabulary such as 'a number' and 'inconsistencies'). The tone is more neutral. This is typical of academic written text. In contrast, when speaking in academic settings as in text B we can be more informal, using 'I' and more everyday vocabulary like 'a lot'. This is acceptable in a tutorial or seminar situation.

ACADEMIC ENGLISH

Features of academic written style:

- Your writing should be objective and neutral, avoid using strongly emotional or informal language. For example: 'After the war the country faced a number of serious problems', not 'After the war the county was in a mess'.
- Avoid personal pronouns (unless you are writing a reflection). Say: 'This paper will argue that . . .', not 'I think . . .'. Avoid contractions (it's) and informal abbreviations such as 'etc.'.
- The passive voice can be used to make writing sound more objective and formal.

EXAMPLE ESSAY

In this paper for a Masters in Business Administration subject, the student was asked to reflect on his own personal development. The first part is an academic essay and the second part is a personal reflection on the writer's growth in light of the theory. It contains personal pronouns like 'I' – this is not common in academic writing. Comments on paragraph structure and the conclusion are included in italics.

Personal Experience, Locus of Control and the Development of Virtue

A key aspect of becoming a leader capable of managing and leading across cultures is the capacity to know oneself, both strengths and weaknesses.

This sentence establishes the context for the discussion.

Reflecting on personal experience in the light of new ideas and theoretical frameworks provides a powerful tool for doing this.

This sentence provides more detailed information about the context.

This paper examines the relationship between personal experience, locus of control and the development of virtue and argues that they are closely inter-related. It draws on both theoretical concepts, and the author's own life story.

These sentences identify the main themes for the paper.

It argues that there is a strong relationship between personal experience, locus of control and the development of virtue.

This sentence states the writer's argument.

The essay will begin by defining these key concepts then the relationship between them will be argued with reference to both theory and personal experience.

This sentence outlines the sequence in which the author will present his ideas.

Personal experience is the ongoing accumulative consequence of being in situations, observing through the senses and being aware. It is a subjective and personalised lens that influences the way in which an individual looks at the world. Winnicott (1960) explores this concept using the interpersonal context of the mother–child dyad (<http://members.tripod.com/~jonmills/Dasein.htm>). In this framework, personal experience starts from the infant's capacity to recognise and enact spontaneous needs for self-expression. However, this is contingent on the responsiveness of the 'good-enough mother' within an appropriate 'holding environment'.

According to Winnicot (1965), a holding environment is created when a child feels emotionally and physically safe when 'contained by an adult'. Accordingly, the etiology i.e. the framework of why things occur is contingent on the quality of maternal responsiveness. Thus, a mother can choose to either strengthen an infant's sense of omnipotence or not.

Overall, personal experience is an iterative form of programming that builds wordless emotional blueprints based on the responses and results of past interaction. This point is supported by Goleman's (1995) notion of emotional intelligence. Such blueprints will also be in part determined by personality and disposition.

Rotter's (1966) theory related to locus of control classifies personality dispositions depending upon the individual's belief that rewards or reinforcements result from personal actions and skills (internal locus of control) or from factors outside of oneself (external locus of control). People who believe in external factors such as luck, fate, powerful others or destiny may not display the same resilience that people who believe in their ability to control their own destinies will.

In this context, McCombs confirms the intrinsic possibility of changing one's locus of control. McCombs asserts that 'the degree to which one chooses to be self-determining is a function of one's realization of the source of agency and personal control'. Thus, an individual can choose to feel energised about accomplishment or feel daunted by feelings of inadequacy. A useful notion for considering such an issue is the timeless concept of virtue.

Aristotle believed that by reasoning well, human beings can live well and this was his definition of happiness. Doing anything well requires virtue or excellence, and therefore, in order to live well, the rational soul will need to engage in activities that are in accordance with virtue or excellence (*Stanford Encyclopaedia* 2006).

Aristotle's definition of virtue is open ended. Whilst decrying certain emotions and actions such as envy and theft as being wrong always, he held that ethics cannot be dissolved to a set of rules. Human beings have the potential to become ethically virtuous by going through two stages: by developing proper habits during their childhood; and then, when their reason is fully developed, they must acquire practical wisdom. This does not imply that one must first fully acquire the ethical virtues, and then, at a later stage, add on practical wisdom. Ethical virtue is fully developed only when it is combined with practical wisdom. This starts from situations in childhood that call for appropriate actions and emotions. As we rely less on others and develop our own thinking, we learn to create a larger picture of human life, our deliberative skills improve, and our emotional responses are perfected. Consequently, ethical virtue enables a good person to successfully discover what is best in each situation. This facilitates the achievement of an individual's happiness as defined earlier.

According to Winnicott's theory, the plaintive cry of a new-born baby sets off causation and is the start of several antecedents during the course of a person's life. Over time, the baby forms its own notions of its behaviour and the typical responses that are triggered at the other end. As the baby grows up, this filter of personal experience is influenced by each interaction with the external environment, social and cultural values and personality types. Thus, each cumulative personal experience appears to influence an individual's capacity to respond to and interact with the external environment, i.e. impact internal or external locus of control in some measure.

Although there is relatively little research on how locus of control beliefs develop, there is evidence that cultural and social factors play important roles (Battle and Rotter 1963; Graves 1961). Lefcourt (1966, p. 32) summed up the findings relating to locus of control and ethnic and socioeconomic variables as, '. . . perhaps the apathy and what is often described as lower-class lack of motivation to achieve may be explained as a result of the disbelief that effort pays off'.

In this regard, Seligman (1991) affirms that locus of control manifests itself as optimism or pessimism in people.

In this sentence the author links to the previous paragraph with the phrase 'in this regard' and then gives the topic of the paragraph: the relationship between locus of control optimism and pessimism.

There appears to be an inter-related relationship between experience and attitudes of optimism or pessimism. In Seligman's view, pessimism, although seeming to be so deep rooted as to be permanent, can in fact be changed by applying the principles of learned optimism. This, in turn, will have an impact on the outcome of future events and, thereby influence the locus of control.

In these two sentences the author further explores the topic.

Overall, experience is not the only contributory factor to the development of the locus of control.

In this final sentence of the paragraph the author introduces the notion of experience which leads into the next paragraph.

Aristotle emphasised that the practice and development of virtue was concurrent with personal experience. He likened the practice of virtue to be akin to a skill in performing a complex and difficult activity. In following the path of virtue, by deciding what to do, a person would not have to contend with internal pressures to act otherwise. This eliminates the desire to do something that is considered to be shameful; and there will be no undue distress at having to give up a pleasure, once there is a realisation of the need to forego. This implies that a person following Aristotle's definition of virtue will need to have a high internal locus of control based on self-discipline. Only then will it be possible to practice a virtuous lifestyle that is centred on moral reasoning.

The above theoretical argument indicates a relationship between experience, locus of control and virtue. Experience does impact on the locus of control. However, there appears to be overwhelming evidence, based on the work of Seligman, that experience is not the only contributory factor to locus of control. In other words, locus of control can be changed through modification of the underlying attitude.

Aristotle's definition of virtue implies the need for a high internal locus of control if one is to remain steadfast to one's virtues. Aristotle also emphasised the role of experience in shaping and influencing the development of virtue.

This paper will now reflect on my own personal growth in the light of the above established relationship between experience, locus of control and virtue.

As a child born in the 1960s, I was brought up in a traditional middle-class Hindu family. My parents' interpretation of Hindu karma was akin to Seligman's principle of learned helplessness. They believed that our actions are pre-determined by our past karma from a previous birth. This explains the fluctuations in our life and our inability to control the events in our lives. This philosophy was the backdrop of the first four decades of my life. I meandered through university, post graduate education and worked for many years. I was in a situation where I let myself be influenced by others' perception that I was having a great career. All this while, dissatisfaction was building up.

In my personal life, there was the intense trauma of losing both my parents and a failed relationship. I was pushed into a corner as I was only allowed limited visitation rights to my daughter whom I loved very much. My health deteriorated considerably. I was embittered by all of these experiences. The inference was that life was meaningless and without hope. My experiences seemed to validate my early conditioning that one's destiny was uncontrollable. Clearly, I had created a strong sense of external locus of control for myself by the turn of the last century.

It was at this point in time that I began a new relationship. With my partner's support, I got a sense of hope and developed inner belief. I realised that my foremost virtue was to be authentic and that I had been anything but that in the past. As I felt more and more empowered, I decided to break out of my environment. Alien as it was in my culture to pursue higher education in middle age, I decided to relocate to Australia in the year 2004. I had always wanted to study for an MBA. By shifting my attitude from external to internal locus of control, I created this opportunity in order to embrace my own sense of authenticity.

The experience of living overseas and studying over the last year has not only enriched my intellect but also supported the authentic nurturing of my nature. My earlier experiences in life strongly influenced my locus of control and inhibited the development of authenticity.

However, by means of a change in the underlying attitude, I have been able to shift my locus of control in a manner that supports the development of my personal virtue of authenticity. I feel more empowered and energised now. I believe that this will also influence the outcome of my experiences in future whilst contributing to the sense of happiness in being true to myself.

Conclusion

In conclusion theoretical frameworks exploring personal experience, locus of control and the development of virtue, confirm the inter-relationship between the three concepts.

Summary of key points in paper.

A baby's experience is the starting point in the life-long conditioning of the locus of control and has a bearing on the development of virtue. However, a concrete goal of virtuous happiness and the emotional orientation of self belief (internal locus of control) will also enable the creation of a meaningful personal experience. As Aristotle profoundly observed 'Virtue makes the goal right, practical wisdom the things leading to it'.

Relates back to his central idea.

The experiences of my own life illustrate both dimensions of the inter-relationship brought out above.

Refers to central argument.

Overall, there appears to be compelling support for the strong relationship between personal experience, locus of control and the development of virtue.

Concluding sentence.

References

Battle, E.S. and Rotter, J.B. (1963), 'Children's feelings of personal control as related to social class and ethnic group', *Journal of Personality*, **31**, 482–90.

Goleman, D. (1995), *Emotional Intelligence*, London: Bloomsbury.

Graves, T.D. (1961), 'Time perspective and the deferred gratification pattern in a tri-ethnic community', PhD dissertation, University of Pennsylvania.

Lefcourt, H.M. (1966), 'Internal versus external control of reinforcement: a review', *Psychological Bulletin*, **65**, 206–20.

Rotter, J.B. (1966), 'Generalized expectancies for internal versus external control of reinforcement', *Psychological Monographs*, **80** (1), 1–28.

Seligman, M.E.P. (1991), *Learned Optimism*, Sydney: Random House.

Stanford Encyclopedia of Philosophy (2006), http://plato.stanford.edu/entries/aristotle-ethics/#4. Accessed 26 March 2009.

Winnicot, D. (1965), *The Maturational Processes and the Facilitating Environment: Studies in the Theory of the Emotional Development*, New York: International Press. http://members.tripod.com/~jonmills/Dasein.htm. Accessed 26 March 2009.

(Adapted with permission from an essay by Moahan Ananda Venkatesan.)

WRITING ACTIVITIES

Find an academic text, for example a textbook or journal article; if you have your course outline, go to the recommended reading:

1. Highlight the introduction, the first sentence of each paragraph and the conclusion. What is the writer's argument or main point? Underline and note useful linking words.
2. How does the author integrate work from other writers? Do they use direct or indirect quotes? What is the purpose of the quote? What reporting verbs are used?
3. Keep a journal. Writing improves with practice. Write as often as you can about your experiences and what you are reading. For example after reading for an hour, write a summary of the main ideas in what you have read. Attach this to the article you have read.

RESOURCES FOR ACADEMIC WRITING

Reporting Verbs

These are the verbs you use to introduce someone else's words or research. Make sure you use the appropriate tense and grammar.

For example:

'This research <u>demonstrates</u> the difference between . . .'. The present tense is used here to give facts. The present tense is commonly used in reporting verbs.
'Earlier research <u>demonstrated</u> that there was little difference.' The use of the past tense here suggests that there has been a change in the way the research is viewed.

The following reporting verbs may be used for presenting neutral or factual information:

- Add.
- Ask.

- Conclude.
- Consider.
- Demonstrate.
- Explore.
- Illustrate.
- List.
- Note.
- Observe.
- Show.
- State.
- Suggest.

For example: 'Smith (2010) <u>demonstrates</u> the importance of under-standing the causes of the problem and <u>suggests</u> that scientists consider alternative research methods.'

Use these verbs for presenting information more strongly:

- Argue.
- Advocate.
- Condone.
- Deny.
- Encourage.
- Highlight.
- Object.
- Postulate.
- Propose.
- Recommend.
- Reject.
- Support.
- Stress.

For example: Advocates of this method such as Mackay (2009) <u>argue</u> strongly in favour of a change in legislation.

Common Errors

It is important to learn how to proofread your own word by looking out for common errors such as the ones which follow.

Grammar: incorrect subject–verb agreement

Usually a singular subject needs a singular verb and a plural subject a plural verb: 'The solutions to this problem ~~is~~ are expensive'

Uncountable nouns, for example information, research, advice, knowledge, experience usually have a singular verb, for example: 'Research <u>suggests</u> that this approach could be beneficial.'

Some noun phrases, for example with the verb + ing, may contain a plural noun but will still have a singular verb, for example: 'Establishing clear guidelines <u>is</u> critical to success.'

Grammar: mistakes with verb endings

They can ~~calculated~~ calculate . . .
It had been ~~establish~~ established . . .

Grammar: commonly confused verbs: rise/rose/risen; raise/raised/raised

'*The prices <u>rose</u>*' (verb has no object).
'*The director <u>raised</u> their salary*' (verb has an object in this case the salary).

Grammar: incorrect use of articles (a, an, the)

Use <u>a</u> with countable nouns that begin with a consonant or consonant sound, for example: a car, a list, a European, a university.
Use <u>an</u> before countable nouns that begin with a vowel or silent 'h', for example: an error, an idea, an hour.
Use <u>the</u> when an object is one of a kind or being referred to specifically: 'The winner is . . .';
'The woman I met last week'.

Vocabulary: Commonly confused words

Economic: related to the economy
Economics: study of the economy
Economical: good value for money
'The GDP is an example of an ~~economical~~ economic indicator.'
Another/other
'~~Other~~ objective of this research . . .'. This should be: The other/another objective of this research . . .'.

NOTE

*   The authors would like to acknowledge the assistance over many years of the Language and Learning team at Queensland University of Technology, Brisbane, Australia.

REFERENCES AND FURTHER READING

Bailey, S. (2006), *Academic Writing: A Handbook for International Students*, London: Routledge.

Brick, J. (2008), *Academic Culture: A Student's Guide to Studying at University*, Sydney: National Centre for English Language and Research.

Burnapp, D. (2009), *Getting Ahead as an International Student* (electronic resource), Maidenhead: McGraw-Hill International (UK).

Kean, T. and L. Hamilton (2008), 'Send more US students abroad', *Christian Science Monitor*, 12 June.

Lawson, L., P. Nelson and M. Reese (2004), *Becoming a Writer at University*, Brisbane: QUT.

Morley-Warner, T. (2009), *Academic Writing Is: A Guide to Writing in the University Context*, Sydney: Association for Academic Language and Learning.

Starfield, S. and B. Paltridge (2007), *Thesis and Dissertation Writing in a Second Language: A Handbook for Supervisors*, London: Routledge.

Swales, J. and C. Feak (1994), *Academic Writing for Graduate Students*, Ann Arbor, MI: University of Michigan Press.

Useful Websites

http://www.phrasebank.manchester.ac.uk/critical.htm (accessed 1 March 2010). This is an excellent phrasebook of academic vocabulary and sentence stems.

http://www.monash.edu.au/lls/llonline/index.xml (accessed 1 March 2010). This website from Monash University provides excellent examples of most types of academic writing and extensive online tutorials.

http://owl.english.purdue.edu/ (accessed 1 May 2010). This website from the online writing lab at Purdue University in the USA is one of the best academic writing websites available. It covers a wide range of topics including grammar and plagiarism.

http://www.arts.yorku.ca/caw/resources.html (accessed 1 May 2010). The University of York Centre for Academic Writing has many valuable resources; see its academic writing guide.

http://www.utoronto.ca/writing/index.html (accessed 1 May 2010). The University of Toronto provides many detailed pages on academic reading and writing (for example critical analysis). See their Frequently Asked Questions.

10.   Communication: speaking in the global classroom

WHY IS SPEAKING IN THE GLOBAL CLASSROOM SO IMPORTANT?

Good communication skills in both your first and second language are vital to your future career success. Take a look at the jobs advertised on your favourite employment website. You will see that for most jobs in the global marketplace you will need to communicate well in both speaking and writing. You will need to present your ideas confidently in a range of situations such as in front of a small group or a large group. You will find that colleges and universities seek to develop these skills through a range of activities such as in class presentations or discussions in tutorials. These can range from five minutes to up to an hour in postgraduate or final-year studies. If you have conducted research, as in a masters or doctoral programme, your final oral presentation of your work is a key part of your assessment. Oral presentations may be individual or part of a group presentations. In tutorials, for example, a case meeting may be simulated where you discuss a problem or conduct a case analysis.

By giving a presentation or participating in a tutorial, you will not only gain a better understanding of content knowledge but you will also learn how to discuss ideas and present your point of view, ask questions and answer questions. Giving a presentation of a topic requires you to understand your subject deeply and to be able to distil key points and to memorize these in order to communicate them in a powerful but simple manner. It is thus an excellent learning tool.

Although written assessment and exams are still the most common form of assessment, your spoken communication will also be used to assess your understanding of a topic and may contribute to your final grade. Your tutorial participation may also receive a percentage of your final grade, particularly in subjects like law. Even if there is no grade for speaking in tutorials, remember that being able to communicate well will help you to make the best of any group work you are asked to do. This chapter will provide an overview of the types of speaking you will have to do both as part of a group and as a presenter. It will give you an idea of some of the challenges you may face and discuss how you can improve your speaking.

SOME OF THE CHALLENGES OF SPEAKING UP IN CLASS AND STRATEGIES FOR IMPROVING YOUR PERFORMANCE

> International students have so much to contribute, but unless they speak up in class we cannot assess this. (University lecturer)

Speaking up in class can be a challenge for all students. However it is especially difficult if you are speaking in a second language and if you come from an educational background where student participation is not encouraged. This section will address some of the reasons why speaking up can be difficult, and the following section will suggest some strategies to help increase participation.

I Don't Fully Understand this Topic so it's Better if I Don't Say Anything

Topics discussed at university level are often complex and there may be a number of ways to answer questions about the area. Remember no one expects you to understand every aspect of the topic. One of the purposes of a tutorial class is to enable you to ask questions and to learn more about the topic from speaking with your tutor and your peers. You are expected to show an intelligent interest in the subject and to ask questions to clarify anything that is not clear to you. But you are not expected to understand everything and to know every answer perfectly. Often there is no one right answer but you can give your understanding and interpretation. It is through class participation that you will develop your skills in argument and your capacity to express yourself.

However make sure you are well prepared and that you have read and made notes about key readings and revised your lecture notes so that you are aware of the major areas and points that you need to understand better. It is quite acceptable to say that you have not fully understood something and would like clarification from the group or your tutor. Many students find it helpful to meet with fellow students before the class to discuss readings or problems. You may be able to email your lecturer or tutor to help you better understand a question but try not to use this as a substitute for class participation. You may find that others in the class had the same question and will benefit from the discussion.

I'm Just a Student, the Tutor Should Do the Talking

Across cultures and countries there will be differences in the way the teacher–student relationship is regarded. Students from some cultural backgrounds may find it strange to question the teachers and may feel that they should respect them and just listen because of the tutors or lecturers' higher level of learning or perhaps their age. It is important to respect the contribution of your tutor and all members of your class. However that respect does not mean you have to remain silent. In Western classrooms, tutors consider that a good tutorial is one in which everyone has participated. If you say nothing you may miss opportunities to learn about the topic and extend your language skills. If your participation is being assessed you may indeed lose marks.

I Don't Feel Comfortable Calling my Tutor by their First Name

In English-speaking countries it is usual to call lecturers and tutors by their first name except in very formal situations such as the defence of a thesis or at a conference. If you still feel unsure about this you could check by observing what other students call the lecturer. The tutor or lecturer may also clarify this by saying something like, 'Please call me Carol'.

My English Isn't Good Enough and People Don't Seem to Understand Me

Many students entering university with English as a second language may feel this way as they may have not had a chance to speak English in their home country outside of the classroom. They lack confidence. To build your confidence, seek out opportunities to speak with class mates and people you meet in your daily life. Make yourself aware of topics people tend to talk about (for example sports events, local issues) and be prepared to start conversations with others. One good way to build confidence in your speaking skills is to join a club or society; check your university for suggestions. Your university may also offer activities such as conversation clubs and language exchange that will help you build confidence in speaking. You may feel you simply do not have time to talk to other students and to make new contacts inside and outside the university. It is also very easy to mix mostly with people from your own country. That is understandable, but if you do this you may miss out on a once-in-a-lifetime opportunity to develop your second language.

You may find that people do not understand you the first time as they are not familiar with your accent. Be prepared for this and use strategies such as noting down a word or using an example. To improve your pronunciation become aware of your own areas of difficulty, that is, where others find it hard to understand you. It could be a particular sound or the stress pattern in a key word. There are many resources to help you improve your pronunciation; some suggestions are given at the end of this chapter.

'I Don't Like Talking in Front of Others. In My Country We Say Silence is Golden.' (Taiwanese Postgraduate Student)

Personal conversation styles are different. There will be some (both international students and those studying in their own country) who prefer to keep quiet and listen while others do the talking. There are two issues here: it is not the amount you say that will show you have understood and are participating, you can show you have understood and are interested with your body language and by asking a good question. However, confidence in speaking in front of others is a key skill for you to develop for your future career and you should try to take every opportunity to practice it. To improve your spoken English you need to participate in conversation.

The Other Students Speak so Fast I Can Never Find an Opportunity to Speak

Many international students find the pace and style of English-speaking students very intimidating; they can find it is hard to get a word in! It may seem as if there may never be a quiet or perfect moment for you to put your comment in. It is important that you learn to manage yourself in such situations. Use body language to signal that you are ready to say something and practice the phrases you can use to introduce what you have to say. For further suggestions see the section at the end of this chapter.

Tutorials

A lecture is still a very common way in which a course will deliver information about a topic to a large number of students. Tutorials are smaller classes where students work with a tutor to explore and better understand the material presented in a lecture. It could involve:

- A round table discussion of questions or a reading or case study.
- A student or group of students being asked to present a topic or reading and lead discussion. In some subjects you will have a specific role such as reporter or leader.

A tutorial is typically held after a lecture and lasts around 50 minutes. Your attendance may be voluntary or you may receive marks for attending. Even if no mark is attached to your attendance, it is strongly recommend that you attend all tutorials as you will gain helpful insights not only into subject matter but also on how to tackle assignments and exams.

In some subjects you may receive a grade for your participation; you may also be asked to present a topic, and this will be graded. Read your course outline and any marking criteria carefully for details of this. Do not hesitate to speak to your tutor if you have any questions about this.

STRATEGIES FOR SUCCESS

Tutor Expectations

Your participation in tutorials is a vital part of your time at university: your participation may be rated and this contributes to your overall assessment. A tutorial is a good place to get to know other class members but also to understand your tutor's expectations. They may well be marking your assignment.

You should:

- Attend all tutorials, workshops and seminars.
- Be prepared, for example do the reading assigned or in a case study know the facts of a case.
- Prepare tutorials carefully by reading and making a note of possible comments, questions or examples. Re-read your lecture notes from just before the tutorial.
- Know key words and maybe the names of key authors (you could practice saying these names).
- Show you understand or are beginning to understand principles and concepts.
- Listen to others.
- Ask relevant questions.
- Answer or attempt to answer relevant questions raised by others.
- Agree or disagree appropriately.
- Be able to clarify vague answers.
- Plan to say at least one thing each tutorial. Start with very simple things, for example the facts of the case progressing to more challenging issues.
- Do not leave it until week five to hear your own voice in the group.

If you are very nervous about participating, consider the following approach.

Progressive Participation

Each week try to do one of the following:

- Find a chance to say yes or agree with the tutor or participant.
- Summarize a key point about the topic, for example reading or case (try to do this early in the class).
- Find a chance to make a comment on something someone says.
- Use active listening techniques. It can be helpful to paraphrase something that is said to check your understanding. Useful opening gambits are:
  - ○ 'Let me see if I understand what you are saying . . .'
  - ○ 'So what you are saying is . . .'
- Remember that posture and eye contact show you are listening.
- Prepare (write down) a comment thought or a question on your reading. Find a place to make this comment, for example 'She makes an interesting point in section . . .'.
- If you disagree with something you have read, say so, but write down what you want to say and anticipate counter-arguments.

Learn from Others

- Get to know your tutors. It is easier to talk to someone you already know.
- If possible try to meet with members of the group before or after the tutorial to discuss issues and to chat. This will help you to feel more comfortable in front of the group.
- Observe and make a note of how more confident students express themselves, for example how they agree, disagree, interrupt, ask for clarification. Use one of these expressions in your next tutorial.

Remember that all students, domestic and international, are under pressure to perform well in tutorials, and try not to be discouraged by abrupt comments.

Body Language and Pace

You also participate with your body language. Try to be open and friendly and show this in your body language. Smile where appropriate, look interested, nod, make eye contact briefly with the person you are speaking to. All these things communicate that you are participating just as much as the language you use. Keep an open posture, for example keep your hands open, try not to cross your arms defensively.

Remember, the discussion may be fast and quite difficult to enter so when you have something to say, get ready to say it before the next person has finished, lean forward in your chair and use a sentence stem like those listed at the end of the chapter to begin making your contribution.

PRESENTATIONS

Increasingly at university you will be asked to give your ideas orally in the form of a presentation. While this may be challenging, it is an excellent way to develop your understanding of a topic. It will also build confidence for future job interviews and for your professional life.

How Long is a Typical Presentation?

Presentations vary in length, for example from ten minutes in an undergraduate course to 40 minutes in a postgraduate presentation, or one hour in the defence of a PhD. It could be an individual presentation or part of a group presentation.

Purpose of Your Presentation

Part of the purpose of a presentation is to show that you have a confident mastery of your subject area. However, just as with academic writing it is rare that you will simply be communicating information. Your presentation will usually involve analysis and you should be able to argue your case persuasively based on the research and reading you have undertaken.

Above all it is vital to understand what is expected of you, so it is essential to read the question and marking criteria thoroughly. You should know who your audience is and how much they understand about your topic. You will need to make a careful selection of points according to the purpose of your presentation and your audience.

Spoken and Written Language

If you are adapting your presentation from an essay you have done, you may need to completely rewrite it in simpler spoken English. Your aim will be to engage your audience by presenting your ideas in strong but simple language.

ACTIVITY

Compare the two sections given below, one spoken, one written. Which of these features of academic style do they have?

Features of academic style

- Hedging/tentativeness (careful to show that there are many sides to the question and that the argument the writer has presented is open to debate).
- Analysis of issues.
- Use of evidence (for example facts and references).
- Formal language (for example less use of personal pronouns and abbreviation, less colourful language, use of passive and more formal vocabulary).

Spoken

You have to ask yourself why there has been such an exponential rise in this in the past 25 years to become the number 1 childhood mental diagnosis. Why in a wealthy and educated part of society with its centre in the USA, but rising fast in Australia, are there so many children afflicted with ADHD. Cohen has called it the 'full scale psychiatric colonization of childhood'. First let me make it clear that I absolutely agree that ADHD can wreck lives. It is not a simple black and white issue. But you have to ask yourself what is driving this increase in doctors' diagnosing ADHD.

Written

It is not clearly understood why in the past 25 years there has been a rapid rise in Attention Deficit Hyperactivity Disorder (ADHD) diagnoses among children, making it now the most prevalent childhood mental illness diagnosis. The US Centre for Disease Control estimates that 8.4 per cent of American children have been diagnosed with ADHD (Parens 2009). Similar trends are found in other countries including Australia (APS 2007). Some critics have called this 'full scale psychiatric colonization of childhood' (Cohen 2007). The disabling impacts of ADHD are not disputed; however the focus of this paper is on the factors associated with the increasing diagnosis of ADHD and whether ADHD, particularly among children, is being over diagnosed.

Notes
Both texts are tentative, analytical and use evidence, but the spoken text uses slightly less formal expression (for example 'You have to ask yourself' compared with 'It is not clearly understood why . . .') and more colourful, less neutral language (for example 'exponential' compared with 'rapid'; 'can wreck lives' compared with 'disabling impacts'.

Content

Just as you need to choose an appropriate style, care also needs to be taken to select content carefully in light of what the task requires (see your marking criteria) and who your audience is. Ask yourself: does this idea relate well to the topic and will the audience follow my message?

Structure

No matter how short your presentation, it is vital that you keep to a simple, clear structure. Begin by analysing your topic and researching your presentation. Analyse the key issues and develop your argument. Keep in mind how you will open and conclude. Consider how many minutes you have (typically allow about 150 words per minute) and begin to plan the introduction, body and conclusion. Many people find it helpful to write out the speech word for word.

Introduction (roughly 10 per cent of the presentation)

- Should help you capture the attention of your audience.
- Gives some more background information and communicates the importance of your topic.
- Gives an overview or plan of your presentation. It tells the audience how and what you are going to tell them.

Body

- Should be carefully structured, for example around major themes.
- There should be clear links between sections.

- Use transition words and signpost words showing what you have just talked about and what you will talk about next. For example, 'So we have looked at some of the causes, now let's look at some strategies for change'. At the end of the chapter there is a list of these transition words.

Conclusion (about 25 per cent of your presentation)

- Review your main points, highlighting key facts and arguments.
- Do not introduce any major new points.
- Draw implications from what you have talked about, for example make a prediction or recommendation.
- Thanks and questions.

Opening and Closing Techniques

The opening and closing of your presentation are the parts which people will remember best. So it is important to plan these well. Practice these as much as you can so that you almost know them by heart, including your gestures and body language with your slides.

- Opening. Create a bridge to the audience with an interesting fact, statistic, story, news item, visual or question.
- Closing. Sum up your points. Practice intonation of key words. Maybe include another quotation to conclude. Practice getting your timing right, as a presentation can be spoiled if you run out of time and fail to conclude decisively.

Preparation

> I took two USB pen drives with my PowerPoint presentation to the conference, neither worked. Fortunately I had emailed it to myself and could retrieve it that way. (Conference presenter)

The following suggestions will help you prepare well:

- Write your speech out.
- Check the pronunciation of key words, check where the stressed syllables are in these words, practice these words.
- Prepare simple large notes of key points, your transition words and places where you need to pause and look at the audience.
- Practice it until you know it very well, but do not recite it.
- Practice in a large room – try to project your voice across the room.

- Practice with friends.
- Double-check your technology and always have a backup plan.

Non-verbal Communication

Non-verbal communication is a vital part of your presentation. Albert Mehrabian (1971) claims that we are influenced:

- First, by what we see: for example appearance and behaviour of the speakers, images presented.
- Next, by the tone of the voice: a flat tone creates a lack of interest; an enthusiastic tone can make even a potentially dry topic of interest.
- And then, by the content of what is being said.

You may have a well-researched and prepared paper, but your appearance, posture, gestures and facial expression, lack of eye contact (for example if you simply read your speech) with your audience may detract from your paper. Similarly if your tone of voice is flat, it will be difficult to maintain interest.

Delivery

> When I give a presentation I say to myself I know this subject, I want to be here, I have something to tell you and I want to want to tell you. (Thai Masters in Communication student)

Your aim should be to make your presentation as interesting as possible. Be enthusiastic. Engage with your audience and talk to them about your topic. You cannot be engaging if you are not confident about your speech. Do not read your speech as this means you will find it difficult to engage with the audience as you cannot make eye contact with them. To develop confidence, prepare well, using the points below to guide you.

Suggestions for delivery

Appearance:

- Dress in a tidy and professional manner.

Posture:

- Practice in front of a mirror or film yourself.
- Correct nervous mannerisms.

- Don't hug your arms around yourself.
- Make welcoming gestures with open hands.
- Stand straight and face your audience.
- Don't hide your face or touch your face and hair.

Facial expression:

- Smile and look interested but don't feel you need to smile all the time.

Eye contact:

- At the start and from time to time, look across the room slowly; try to include most people.
- If you are very nervous, find a friendly face to return to.
- When asked a question, make eye contact before answering the question.

Voice:

- Not too soft or too fast.
- Use a positive, enthusiastic voice and intonation.
- Vary your speed, pause.

Problems:

- If you lose your place and don't know how to continue, do not panic, take a deep breath and go to the next heading; your audience may not even notice.

Answering Questions

Prepare the types of questions you think people could ask, and answer these. If it is a group presentation, decide who will answer. If you do not understand a question, ask the person to rephrase it. If you are still unsure what is meant you could suggest that the questioner speaks to you at the end of the session. You are not usually expected to know the answer to every question; you can say, 'I'm not sure I know the answer to that question, does anyone have any suggestions?' Stay polite and positive.

Group Presentations

- Divide the task up logically and realistically. Practice together and make sure you have a system to respect the amount of time allocated.
- Show your teamwork with clear language signposts. For example: 'I've given a brief situational analysis, Kim will now talk about the decisions we made.'
- Use non-verbal gestures that are inclusive of other team members, for example a smile, helping each other if there is a problem.

After the Presentation: What Could I Have Done Better?

Being able to reflect on and learn from experience is a characteristic of successful learning. A few hours after your presentation, it is a good idea to assess your progress using the SWOT method. For example, ask yourself the following questions:

Strengths

- What did you do well in this presentation?
- Which sections did you feel worked best?
- Why?

Weaknesses

- Where did you communicate less well?
- Was it your delivery? For example, were you so nervous that you couldn't engage with the audience?
- Was there a problem with scope? For example did you have too much or too little to say?

Opportunities
Reflecting on the above, what can you do in your next presentation to improve?

Threats
If you still feel very uncomfortable with your presentation skills, put in place some strategies to improve, for example: extensive practice; join a speaker's club such as Toastmasters; attend some training sessions; and consult the learning support services at your university. (Adapted from Burns and Sinfield 2007.)

LANGUAGE FOR TUTORIAL PARTICIPATION

The following sentence stems could be help you to make some comments in tutorials.

Making a Comment

- One thing that struck me was . . .
- What I found interesting in this article was . . .
- The idea was interesting but the research design was weak.
- One aspect I found hard to understand was . . .

Asking For an Opinion or For Clarification

- What do you think he means here?
- Why do you think the author has said this?
- I'm not really sure what this section meant . . .
- Could you explain this . . .

Interrupting

- I'd like to say something here . . .
- Mmm, could I say something?

Agreeing/Disagreeing

- I agree . . .
- Exactly . . .
- Right . . .
- Look, I agree with you up to a point, but . . .
- I understand what you're saying, but don't you think it could also be . . .

LANGUAGE FOR PRESENTATIONS

To help listeners follow, good speakers clearly signal to their audience:

- the structure of their talk;
- when they move between parts of their talk;
- really important points (for example data) and relationships between these points.

The following phrases can be used to do this. Make sure to highlight these words on your notes; they are really vital, especially if the audience is unfamiliar with your topic or your accent. Also remember to pause at key points to highlight important information that you have said or are about to say.

Introducing Structure

- First . . .
- Next . . .
- To begin with . . .
- Initially . . .

Moving between Points

- Also . . .
- Now we have considered X, now let's look at Y . . .
- So those are some of the issues in X, we shall move on to Y . . .

Concluding

- Finally . . .
- In conclusion . . .
- To sum up . . .

Explaining Cause/Effect

- Consequently . . .
- As a result . . .

Contrasting Ideas

- On the other hand . . .
- Another way of looking at this is . . .

Referring to Evidence

- As you can see from this figure . . .
- Now, have a look at this graph . . .

Handing Over to Another Group Member in a Group Presentation

- I've talked about some of the decisions we made. I'll hand over to my partner who will discuss/give details of our performance outcomes . . .

Tip: As you listen to presentations, take a note of the signal words used by speakers.

REFERENCES AND FURTHER READING

Allan, B. (2009), *Study for Business Management* (electronic resource), Maidenhead: McGraw-Hill International (UK).

Brick, J. (2008), *Academic Culture: A Student's Guide to Studying at University*, Sydney: National Centre for English Language and Research.

Brown, L. (2003), *Speaking to be Understood: English as a First or Second Language* Lanham, MD: Scarecrow Education.

Burns, T. and S. Sinfield (2007), *Essential Study Skills: The Complete Guide to Success at University*, 2nd edition, London: Sage.

Mehrabian, A. (1971), *Silent Messages*, Belmont, CA: Wadsworth Publishing Co.

Useful Resources

http://www.uiowa.edu/~acadtech/phonetics/ (accessed 1 March 2010). This is an excellent resource for anyone wishing to improve their pronunciation. It includes animations and modelling of all English sounds and uses American English examples.

http://www.bbc.co.uk/worldservice/learningenglish/grammar/pron/sounds/ (accessed 21 April 2010). This is another excellent resource for anyone wishing to improve their pronunciation. It includes animations and modelling of all English sounds and uses British English examples.

Hancock, M. (2003), *English Pronunciation in Use*, Cambridge: Cambridge University Press. This is a well-designed and easy to use course in English pronunciation. It includes sound recordings.

http://www.toastmasters.org/ (accessed 1 March 2010). Toastmasters International is a speaking club that provides regular opportunities for you to become a confident public speaker.

11. Success with assessment and examinations

Obviously students who are working in a language that is not their own will have added difficulties when they have to use this language within the limits of a test. Under such pressure they often find their languages getting mixed up: some students report that they start thinking in a jumble of their own language and English. Others say they misread the wording of the instructions or question in their panic, or they write down only those points they can express in English even when they know they are not really answering the question. (Ballard and Clanchy 1997, cited in Ryan 2000)

WHAT IS ASSESSMENT?

The activities at university that cause students the greatest stress are assessments, particularly examinations. These cause stress for a number of reasons:

- They are the way in which you are assessed on how well you have learnt what the curriculum states you should have learnt. Any assessment can cause insecurity as we wonder just how much we have understood and remembered. Failure at assessment items can have a significant impact on self-esteem and the financial resources necessary to complete the qualification you are studying for.
- They are often time-constrained, such as timed examinations. Even when this is not the case, they have to be delivered at a particular time. Time constraints cause anxiety and can be a practical difficulty if you are being examined in a language other than your mother tongue.
- Assessment is increasing complex. In most Western universities assessment is no longer predominantly in examination form at the end of the period of study. Assessment comes in many forms, such as assignments, oral presentations, group activities and a range of different examination types. It is important not to assume that assessment at university will be the same as at your previous educational institution.

There is no way to avoid assessment. What is important is that you understand what is expected of you and that you don't leave preparation to the last moment. This chapter takes you through many of the most common types of assessment used in universities. You may well encounter others. The most important thing is to ask if you do not understand what is required, and then do what is required rather than what you think you know best about.

You will hear many different terms applied to assessment. Often these terms are ignored or not fully understood. This can leave you at a disadvantage because you don't fully understand what is expected of you. This chapter will explore some of the terms used when assessment and examinations are discussed, and explain how to do well at each type of assessment. It will also give you the language to ask questions where you do not understand what is required.

Assessment is not there to catch you out. The lecturers are not trying to trick you. For your qualifications to be worth anything, a certain standard needs to be attained. Assessment is a way of determining whether you have reached the required standard. Assessment needs to be seen in the context of the teaching and learning that has been undertaken during the study period. There should be constructive alignment between instruction, learning and assessment (Gulikers et al. 2004; Biggs 2003). This means that the assessment should test what you have been taught.

Assessment can try to measure a number of different things, such as knowledge, skills or understanding. It can provide feedback to you on how you are doing. It can provide feedback to the teacher on how the students are doing. Often any assessment piece is doing a number of these things (Duncan and Noonan 2007). You need to understand what exactly the assessment is trying to measure. Is it checking your content knowledge? Is it measuring how well you can do something or your attitude to a particular idea? Is it measuring how well you understand concepts and can apply them to real-world situations? Understanding what is being measured can help you be successful in each assessment item. As we go through the various types of assessment, tips will be provided on how to decide what the assessment item is trying to measure and how to produce the best possible results.

FORMATIVE AND SUMMATIVE ASSESSMENT

Assessment is frequently described as either formative or summative. Formative assessment occurs during the semester, while summative assessment usually comes at the end of the learning period. Assessment is part of the learning process and many of the assessment items you do will not only measure what you have learnt, but actually be a way of learning. This is particularly true of assignments and projects. Whatever assessment processes are used, they will be aligned with the stated objectives of the course and are likely to focus on the material that the lecturers have emphasized during the teaching period.

Formative assessment can be a very good learning tool and it is worthwhile undertaking any test that you are given even if it is not mandatory. These formative tests can help you learn. The feedback you receive can help you align your learning to what is required and help you improve your strategies for learning effectively. It will give you an idea of how well you understand what is being taught, and provide an opportunity to seek help in areas that are giving difficulties. Formative assessment may also be used to inform the teachers about how you are doing (Frey and Schmitt 2007). The primary benefit of formative assessment is allowing you, the students, to control and improve your own learning. This can be particularly important if you come from a different educational background and if you have different experiences of assessment. Do not assume that what was acceptable in the past will be acceptable in the current situation. Formative assessment provides you with an opportunity to gauge how well you understand the new systems and how well you are absorbing complex ideas, possibly through a foreign language.

Summative assessment has the intention of identifying the extent of your learning. There may be no feedback other than a grade (or mark). It is therefore critical that you understand clearly what is expected of you and how to approach the task of preparation.

Another term that you may hear is 'authentic assessment'. To be authentic the assessment task must reflect the competency that needs to be assessed and represent real-life problems. The thinking processes that experts use to solve the problems in real life are also required by the assessment task (Gulikers et al. 2004) and are therefore an integral apart of authentic assessment. This does not mean that you do not need to understand the theory or do rigorous academic citation, but that you use this theoretical knowledge within a 'real-life' situation. Authentic assessment often takes the form of industry-based projects, work placements or assignments, and requires the application of theoretical understanding to real problems or situations. This can present difficulties if you come from a very different background to the one in which you are studying. Ask for the relevance of a topic or process to be explained.

An authentic task is a problem task that will confront you with activities that are also carried out in professional practice. Understanding the relevance of the task is important. Look for the link to a situation in the real world or working situation and the career you wish to follow.

The goal of authentic assessment is the acquisition of higher-order thinking processes and competencies rather than factual knowledge. This means that authentic assessment is there to find out whether you really understand what you have been taught and are able to use it to solve problems in the 'real world'. This is often very difficult if you have limited experience of the world of work, or if your previous experience has been in a very different context. But nothing is more important. Learning is about more than remembering, and authentic assessment can show you the real difficulties of putting theory into practice.

CRITERION-REFERENCED AND NORM-REFERENCED ASSESSMENT

You may see stated on any course documentation the terms, 'criterion-referenced' or 'norm-referenced'. If these words do not appear, ask which system is being used to mark your assessment item.

Much that is assessed in higher education uses a norm-referencing system. That is, your work is compared with that of other students and the spread of marks reflects comparative ability or knowledge. There is no 'fixed' standard. Your work is compared with how good it is compared to the others in your group.

Criterion-referenced assessment evaluates you against a defined set of objectives or standards, and unlike norm-referenced assessment, does not compare students to each other. Criterion-referenced assessment provides criteria that are used by the lecturer when marking any assessment item. Standards, which should be explained in the course documents, are the level of performance expected. You need to make sure that you are clear about the criteria being used to mark your assessment items. It does not matter how good your work is: if it does not meet the criteria stated you will not do well. Be sure that you address the issues and content that are deemed important by the criteria.

Clear, well-articulated criteria can be a great help to you as they provide a clear direction for your learning. You are not being compared to others. You are assessed for your competence against clearly articulated criteria. Make sure that you are clear what is expected. Seek help to bridge the gap between where you are and where the criteria require you to be. Make sure that you understand what the criteria mean. If you don't understand, ask for clarification.

TYPES OF ASSESSMENT

Assessment is extremely important. You want to pass in your subject and do as well as possible. You may feel disadvantaged because of your lack of background cultural knowledge or experience with particular assessment methods. In earlier chapters you will have read much about critical thinking and how learning happens. What follows here are some guidelines to a tool called Bloom's Taxonomy (Fowler 2004) which is often used to explain the types of learning being measured. For all the assessment items discussed below, there are hints in the question as to the type of learning that is to be measured. Look for these words and they will give you an idea of what the assessment is trying to measure.

- Measuring knowledge. Measuring knowledge is trying to identify what facts, terms and concepts you have learned. The words to look for if the assessment item is measuring knowledge include: who, what, when, where, define, show, recall, select, list. All these are words that seek facts.
- Measuring comprehension. Here you need to demonstrate understanding of facts and ideas. The words to look for if the assessment item is measuring comprehension include: compare, contrast, demonstrate, interpret, explain, illustrate, outline, summarize.
- Measuring application. Here you have to solve problems by applying the knowledge you have acquired, the facts, techniques and rules that you have learned. The words to look for include: apply, choose, develop, make use of, organize, plan, solve, identify.
- Measuring the ability to analyse. Western education puts great store by the ability to analyse. This means that you are able to examine and break down information into its parts by identifying motives or cause, and are able to make inferences from this process and find evidence to support your statements. The words that indicate that analysis is required include: analyse, categorize, classify, compare, examine, distinguish, theme, relationships, assumptions, conclusion.
- Measuring the ability to synthesize. Synthesis means gathering information together in a different way by combining elements in a new pattern, or proposing alternative solutions. The words that indicate that synthesis is required include: build, combine, design, develop, formulate, plan, propose, solve, discuss, adapt, elaborate.
- Measuring the ability to evaluate. Evaluation requires the ability to present and defend opinions by making judgements about

information, the validity of ideas or quality of work based on a set of criteria. The words that indicate that evaluation is required include: conclude, criticize, defend, evaluate, justify, measure, recommend, appraise, opinion, assess.

Each of the types of assessment builds on the one before it. You cannot analyse if you don't have the facts and understand them. The further on in your study you are, the more likely you will be required to move beyond remembering facts and demonstrating your understanding.

With each of the assessment types described below, some of the words above will be used to explain what is expected of you. They will appear in the questions asked and the guidelines given.

Examinations

Written, timed examinations are a traditional means of assessing students in Western business schools. These have typically been handwritten under closed-book, invigilated conditions. No resources were available for the student to call upon. Until recently even translation dictionaries were not allowed. Today the use of laptop computers is increasing, but the principle of 'closed-book' timed examinations remains the same.

This type of traditional examination does not reflect the ideas of authentic assessment. It is often used to measure knowledge and understanding rather than application or critical thinking. It relies on memory to ensure that you have the knowledge to answer the questions. The restricted time provides little space for thinking or reflection. It appears to favour those who are able to remember and regurgitate data.

Examinations now take on many forms, from multiple-choice questions to responding to a case study. There are closed-book examinations, and open-book examinations where students can bring with them materials they might need to refer to. Open-computer examinations have also presented a challenge as to whether students should be able to access the Internet during their examination, or perhaps even email for information. Once Internet access is provided it is difficult to monitor usage. There are those who argue that in today's world open-computer examinations are 'authentic', as this is how you will face challenges in the workplace. However, open-book examinations raise the spectre of plagiarism, and can make it difficult to know whether the work is really that of the student sitting the examination.

Multiple-choice tests are primarily used in a summative way to differentiate between students and rank them. They are best used to assess knowledge and understanding of facts.

There are some challenges in use of examinations for students for whom English is not their first language. There is the pressure of time. Is the amount of reading required reasonable?

Tips for doing well in examinations

- You cannot learn everything you need to know for an examination the evening before.
- Try not to panic – the exam will relate to material that you have covered during the learning period. If you have learned, you will remember it if you don't panic.
- Try to find a way to relax immediately before the examination.
- Read the questions carefully and highlight or underline the key words.
- Look at the value of each question.
- Work out how much time you have for each question and stick to it. You will get no points for questions you haven't answered at all.
- Check carefully how many questions you have to answer. Often there is a choice.
- One trick that can help in an exam is to read the question and then write down a list of everything that you know about the topic. This then gives you a list of information to write your answer from.
- Start with the question you feel most comfortable with. There is no need to start at the beginning and work through in any particular order.
- Keep your answer clearly structured and aligned to the question. This way the marker can easily find the information he or she is looking for. This is important when you think that the marker may be marking many hundreds of examinations.
- When answering mathematical problems, include all your calculations. Even if your answer is incorrect, the marker can see where you went wrong and you may gain points for your method (Marshall and Rowland 2006).
- If you have a memory lapse in the middle of a question, leave a few pages, go onto another question and then come back to the previous question.
- If you run out of time, jot down the main points you were going to make.
- Try to leave time at the end of the exam to read over your answers. Correcting poor expression or spelling, or checking your calculations, can make an important difference. If it is an open-book examination this gives you an opportunity to reference your work, which may be well regarded.

Assignments and Essays

Assignments are commonly used as an assessment method to increase the authenticity of assessment, and bring a connection between theory and the 'real world'. Assignments can take many forms, from theoretical essays to applying theoretical concepts to practical problems, either real or simulated. You may never have written an assignment or essay before so it important that you understand what is required.

Essay or assignment writing outside of the examination context can raise a range of potential difficulties of which you have to be aware. You must remember that Western universities have a very strict view of plagiarism, which is considered intellectual stealing. You may not have found this to be the case with your previous study. You need to ensure that you cite (give credit to) anyone whose idea you use in your assignment. It doesn't have to be a direct quote, but citing the writers that you have drawn your ideas from has many benefits. It shows that you have read the material that is required of you. If you can put your own ideas into the context of what others have said, it shows that you have understood what these writers had to say and well as having ideas of your own.

Don't be tempted to use assignments that you find on the Internet, or the work of other students. There are many ways in which teachers can find out if you have cheated. The technology that helps you, helps them as well. It is also unlikely that any prepared assignment will address the exact requirements of the assignment, giving you poor grades.

Cheating is never worthwhile. Below are some tips for doing well in essays or assignments. There is a lot of work involved in writing a good assignment – give yourself time, and you can feel proud of what you have achieved.

Tips for a good assignment

- Read the assignment question carefully. Highlight the key words that tell you what is required.
- Keep to the word limit. The word 'limit' usually includes any footnotes, but not references.
- Use a recognized referencing system (the one identified by the teacher) and don't forget to ensure that everything cited in the text appears in the reference list at the end of the assignment.
- Start preparing for the assignment well before the submission date. This gives you time to reflect and make changes.
- If you include diagrams, make sure that they are relevant, well labelled, accurately drawn and referenced if they are not original.

- Ask someone to read your assignment to check whether it makes sense to them, and to identify any errors.
- Ensure that your essay is devoid of typographical and grammatical errors. If English is not your first language ask someone to check that your English makes sense.
- Give your essay a clear structure with an introduction and conclusion.
- The essay should stand alone without reliance on appendices, unless otherwise stated.
- Present the evidence carefully and draw your conclusions tentatively. Good critical analysis is key. Make sure that you have stated the facts, the evidence, before stating any opinion or conclusion.

There is a whole chapter on writing that can help you improve the way you present your knowledge and understanding (Chapter 9). These are tips to help you avoid some of the most common mistakes made when submitting assignments and essays.

Case Study

Case study analysis is a popular teaching method but it is also used extensively as an assessment tool. Case studies are used when the teacher wants to develop or measure your capacity to analyse, synthesize and problem-solve. Case studies provide an opportunity for you to relate theory to the problem identified in the case study. Theory remains important but so is your ability to see how that theory is relevant to the situation described. Memory here will not help – it is your ability to demonstrate that you can use the theoretical tools you have to solve a particular problem or understand a particular situation.

Tips for good case study analysis

- Case studies can be used for either examinations or assignments, so the tips associated with these two forms of assessment apply equally to the use of a case study.
- Try to anticipate the type of case study you might get so that you can prepare for the type of questions you might be asked. Review cases that you have done in class.
- Mauffette-Leenders et al. (2001), cited in Dalglish and Evans (2008), suggests a six-step process to use before you start answering any questions:
  - Step 1 – Read the opening and closing paragraphs.
  - Step 2 – Answer the following questions: Who? What? Why? When? How?

○ Step 3 – Have a quick look at any exhibits presented.
○ Step 4 – Quickly review the subtitles in the case – they give you clues about the content.
○ Step 5 – Skim-read the body of the case. If English is not your first language this may take longer than would otherwise be the case. This makes it even more important that you have done steps 1–4.
● Read the questions carefully and reflect.
● Plan your time according to the marks allocated to each question.
● Resist the temptation to digress, and stay focused on exactly what is requested.
● Refer specifically to the case study when answering the questions.

Oral Examinations

Whilst oral examinations are no longer common, presentations are often part of assessment processes. Fluency with language can be a key issue, particularly if the presentation is being given in a second language. It takes considerable confidence to stand up in front of a group of peers to disclose your knowledge and understanding of a topic. However, being able to make a good presentation is critically important in most careers these days. Communication skills are among the most important that you can learn as part of your study, whatever the subject of your degree. Take every opportunity to practice. Like any skill (tennis, chess, surgery), competence comes through practice, not just through understanding.

Chapter 10 deals with spoken communication skills, but below are some tips that apply particularly to presentations as a means of assessment.

Tips for oral presentations

● Be clear about what is being assessed – the content or your presentation skills.
● Even if it is content that is being examined, remember that you can only get marks for what the examiner hears and understands, so your ability to communicate is still important.
● Stick very closely to the time limit given.
● Be very clear about the message you want to give – and that it is the one you have been asked for.
● Identify a few critical pieces of information that you want share.
● Prepare visual aids to support your argument. These must be clear and support what you are saying so they help your message rather than distract from it.

- Prepare a copy of your presentation for the examiner.
- Identify clearly your objectives of your presentation – provide a guide to what you are going to say and the structure of your presentation.
- Speak clearly and do not use unnecessary jargon.
- Remember you are trying to show the examiner how much you know and/or what you can do.
- If it is a group presentation, make sure that it is clear what the contribution of each person is, whether you all speak or not.

Applied Projects

To increase the authenticity of assessment many programs include projects which require students to engage with the 'real world'. You are also often required to work in a group. Some of the special issues associated with group assessment will be considered later, but there are specific considerations where project work is concerned.

If you are a foreign student, projects can present some very real challenges. You may not be familiar with the environment that you are studying in – so may not easily find a real organization to work with. Sometimes work experience, or welcoming organizations, will be arranged by your lecturer, but this is not always the case. If it is a group project, try to join a group that has local contacts – you can learn from them and you will be able to offer a different perspective on what you see in the workplace, and ask questions that others more familiar with the situation might not think to ask. This also means that for domestic students, it would be good to include a foreign student in your group to add to the critical analysis of what you experience.

Tips for a successful workplace project

- In an applied project you have a 'client' as well as an examiner. The client is the organization in which you did your project.
- This may mean that you have two different sets of expectations to meet – the academic ones of the examiner and the applied implications for the 'client' who may also take part in the assessment.
- Whether you are examined orally or through an assignment, you need to use the relevant tips given earlier, but you also need to be aware of these two different sets of expectations.
- In the examination of a workplace project it is important that you still adhere to the highest academic standards with regard to referencing and using the literature rigorously.

- In addition to the academic requirements you need to demonstrate how this theory can help solve the problem presented in the workplace.
- An applied project may often ask for recommendations for the client.
- Make sure that your assessment item relates specifically to the organization in which you worked.
- Do not use jargon or unnecessary technical or academic terms that may not be clear to the client.

Group Assessment

Many students identify that group activities are among the best and the worst of their learning experiences. Where group activities are being assessed, a high level of stress is introduced into the group. Time constraints, inadequate intercultural communication skills and under-developed team skills can cause group assessment to be a stressful and unrewarding process.

Often the reason for group assessment is to develop the capacity in students to work as participating and productive members of a group. This is a skill that you will require in the workplace. There are risks and benefits to being assessed in a group, and many of the issues have been addressed in Chapter 7 on working in groups. However, when the group work is for assessment there are additional pressures, and prejudice for and against different groups or individuals is more likely to come to the fore.

It seems that group assessment is important when group skills are being assessed. If one of the criteria is the nature of the group process, and the roles filled, this makes reflecting on group processes and listening to others part of what has to be achieved.

Tips for being assessed as part of a group

- Ensure that the group understands what the assessment criteria are. Is the assessment measuring content knowledge but using a group format, or are group skills themselves being assessed? Ask if you are not sure.
- Whatever is being assessed, the group interaction will impact on everyone's grades.
- It is not helpful to wish you were in another group. Set out to make the best of the group that you are in. This can best be done by getting to know the group members and their strengths and weaknesses; for example someone who is very shy and perhaps does not speak good English could be very good at data collecting.

- Spend time together at the beginning of the process to get to know each other and to ensure that everyone understand what needs to be done, who is going to do what and the process that is going to be used.
- Also discuss how you are going to deal with problems like free-loading or illness. Your teacher can often help with some rules that you can put in place and most universities have processes to support good group activity.
- Remember that whatever your role in the group assessment, you will be assessed on the product as a whole, so it is in your interests to support your group members to do the best they can.
- Many group assignments provide an opportunity for you to give feedback to the examiner on the work of your peers. Use this opportunity. If you believe that someone has not pulled his/her weight, use this opportunity to provide the feedback. In many cases it will affect his/her grades. Also, if you believe that someone has done a particularly good job, say so.
- Often the grades given for group assignments are a combination of the group mark and individual contribution.

PLAGIARISM

Plagiarism is a contentious issue and one that has the potential to cause great distress to all concerned. Deliberate plagiarism is no more common among international students than among domestic students. However, what is apparent is that if you do not speak English as your first language, you are more likely to get caught. Being caught plagiarizing is not a desirable outcome. Don't plagiarize:

- Find out what the rules are.
- Learn how to reference properly.
- Don't allow others to plagiarize from you – you will be considered equally to blame.

REFERENCES AND FURTHER READING

Ballard, B. and J. Clanchy (1997) *Teaching International Students*, Deakin, ACT: IDP Education Australia.
Biggs, J. (2003), *Teaching for Quality Learning at University*, 2nd edition, Milton Kcynes: Society for Research into Higher Education and Open University Press.

Bloom, J.S. (1965), *The Process of Learning*, Cambridge, MA: Harvard University.

Dalglish, C. and P. Evans (2008), *Teaching in the Global Business Classroom*, Cheltenham, UK and Northampton, MA, USA: Edward Elgar.

Duncan, C.R. and B. Noonan (2007), 'Factors affecting teachers' grading and assessment practices', *Alberta Journal of Educational Research*, **53** (1), 1–21.

Fowler, B. (2004), 'Critical thinking across the curriculum project', Longview Community College, Missouri.

Frey, B.B. and V.L. Schmitt (2007), 'Coming to terms with classroom assessment', *Journal of Secondary Gifted Education*, **18** (3), 402–23, 488, 491.

Gulikers, J.T.M., T.J. Bastiaens and P.A. Kirschner (2004), 'A five dimensional framework for authentic assessment', *Educational Technology, Research and Development*, **52** (3), 67–86.

Marshall, L. and F. Rowland (2006), *Learning Independently*, Frenchs Forest, NSW: Pearson Longman.

Mauffette-Leenders, L.A., J.A. Erskine and M.R. Leenders (2001), *Learning with Cases*, Ontario: Ivey Publishing.

Ryan, Janette (2000), *A Guide to Teaching International Students*, Oxford: OCSLD.

12.   Research students in the global classroom*

GLOBALIZATION OF RESEARCH EDUCATION

More and more students are undertaking a research degree abroad. In recent years in the USA more than 60 per cent of doctoral recipients in science, engineering and economics were born outside the USA (Bound et al. 2009). In addition to PhD programmes, professional doctorates, taught doctorates and European doctorates offer research students many possibilities for international cooperation. The language of postgraduate research is increasingly English, opening many doors for students to work across the globe (Powell and Green 2008).With the integration of research systems within the European Union, there are unprecedented opportunities for researcher mobility within the knowledge triangle of education, research and innovation (European Commission 2009). Likewise in Australia there are many scholarships available for international research students. The following list gives an example of the variety of research being undertaken globally.

- Chinese nursing professor in London investigating best practice for the terminally ill.
- Iranian physicist in Brisbane researching air pollution at airports.
- French engineer in Melbourne modelling attention and road accidents.
- South American physician in Hong Kong studying the spread of infection in hospitals.
- New Zealand executive at INSEAD in Paris determining strategies for introducing new technology.
- German student in South Africa investigating micro-entrepreneurship.
- British student studying European Doctoral Programme in Entrepreneurship and Small Business at the University of Barcelona.

As an international research student you will need to define your topic, establish relationships with your supervisor and colleagues, and conduct, present and write about your research in an unfamiliar environment and probably in a second language. This will certainly be challenging, but as Wright and Cochrane (2000) note, international students are more likely to complete their research degrees successfully than domestic students. Perhaps this is because they have typically invested a huge amount in coming abroad, both personally and financially. They are more likely to be really sure in their own mind about what they hope to achieve by undertaking a research degree and this contributes to their personal strength and capacity to deal with setbacks.

To be a research student abroad is an amazing opportunity. You will meet people who you will collaborate with perhaps for many years, and who will open doors for you in terms of professional networks. Your language and research skills will grow. You will learn to manage complex projects, to set goals and to achieve these goals. You will learn to develop and maintain new, sometimes challenging and maybe difficult relationships with your supervisors and your research team. You will become an expert in your field and will need to negotiate the changes that this will make in the way you relate to your supervisor and your peers. You will need to use all your personal resources: your intellect, and also your interior strengths, for example your capacity to meet challenges. You will need to be resilient and to bounce back after disappointment and setbacks. Most of all you will need to manage yourself and your time, to complete and present your work. You will probably be doing all this in a culture and language which is not your own. This chapter will provide an outline of some of the main issues facing you as an international research student, and make some suggestions for how you can tackle these.

EXPECTATIONS

> Ultimately it's the student's role to complete the project. (African doctoral student)

> You need to be prepared to know your field, to read the literature, to put the time into writing draft after draft; that's what makes research. (Professor Patsy Yates 2008, cited in Lawson 2008)

> It was not an easy experience for me to come to do a PhD. My supervisor said: 'Here's your computer, here's a data base. Get started.' (Saudi Arabian doctoral student)

When you start postgraduate research you will be expected to work as an independent scholar. In addition the way research is conducted in your home university may be very different from the methods used where you are now undertaking your research. This can be the cause of some confusion between the supervisor and a research student. It is important to establish and define what your responsibilities are and how the supervisor sees his/her role. In some projects your supervisor will help you to scope your project and to determine if it is feasible and suitable for the research degree you are undertaking. In other projects you may be working in a very specific, predefined area, perhaps as one part of a larger project. Discussing what your supervisor and the university expect from you and what you expect from them is important. Do this in one of the first meetings with your supervisor.

Use the short questionnaire in Table 12.1 to help you to think about these things. If possible ask your supervisors to do the same questionnaire and use this as a tool to define your respective roles. Rank yourself from 1: I strongly agree this is the supervisor's responsibility to 5: I strongly agree this is the student's responsibility (a score of 3 indicates you feel this is a shared responsibility).

RELATIONSHIPS

Your Supervisor

> Be patient. It can take a long time (up to a year) to learn how to have a good working relationship with your supervisor. (Chinese Doctoral student in nursing)

Forming a good relationship with your supervisor is vital to your success as a research student, and it can be difficult to get right. It is a professional relationship which you need to manage to make it work for you and your project. It will be based on respect for you and for the effort you make, the work you do and the results you achieve. It's quite normal to feel a little shy and uncomfortable at first. As you build your relationship and learn to read your supervisor, you will gain confidence. It will help greatly if you plan your meetings and communication carefully. Certainly he/she is your 'senior', but this does not mean he/she will tell you what to do. It does not mean that you cannot disagree with him/her and challenge what he/she tells you. This may be the case as your understanding of the field grows and you become an expert in your area. You may feel, for example, too shy to ask for clarification. But it is crucial that you become confident to do this.

Research into the successful student–supervisor relationship has found that the supervisor is often a mentor: a professional friend who guides,

Table 12.1   Abstract assessment form

	TOPIC	
1. It is a supervisor's responsibility to select a promising topic.	1 2 3 4 5	It is a student's responsibility to select a promising topic
2. It is the supervisor who decides on the theoretical framework.		A student has the right to decide on his/her own theoretical framework even if conflicts with his/her supervisor.
3. A supervisor should arrange for all facilities, materials and support.		In the end it is a student who must arrange for all facilities, materials and support.
	CONTACT	
4. A supervisor should initiate all meetings with the student.	1 2 3 4 5	A student should initiate all meetings with the supervisor.
5. A supervisor should constantly check the student is working according to plan.		A student should find his/her own way and doesn't need to tell his/her supervisor what he/she is doing.
	WRITING	
6. A supervisor is responsible for the methodology and the content of the thesis.	1 2 3 4 5	A student has total responsibility for ensuring that the methodology and the content of the thesis are appropriate for his/her discipline.
7. A supervisor should assist in the actual writing of the thesis.		Writing the thesis is entirely the responsibility of the student.
8. A supervisor should ask to see drafts of every section to give feedback.		It is up to the student to ask for feedback from supervisors.

Source: Adapted from Moses (1992).

counsels and seeks to develop your knowledge and skills in a particular area (Paltridge and Starfield 2007).

However your supervisor is also your peer, a fellow researcher (Sinclair 2005) and this becomes more and more the case as you move into your second and third year. Take up any opportunity to participate with your supervisor in working groups or to attend conferences or meetings together. You will learn many professional communication and research skills by observing your supervisor.

> I didn't feel comfortable calling my supervisor David, for me in my culture it was a little rude. (Afghan doctoral student in structural engineering)

Sometimes it can be hard to get the relationship right. There can be cultural differences that you will have to understand and negotiate. You may like to give a gift, but don't feel that you have to do this. In Australia, the UK, the USA and Canada it will usually be quite appropriate to use the supervisor's first name. In other countries it would be more usual to use 'Professor' or, for example in France, their title, 'Monsieur/Madame'. The relationship should be friendly but your supervisor may not become a close friend. It will be informal but also professional; you should learn what is appropriate and acceptable in terms of meeting times and asking for help. Learn to become aware of where 'invisible barriers' in terms of space and time may be (Humphrey and McCarthy 1999).

In a series of interviews with PhD students in Australia, students spoke of the need to learn to read their supervisor and to manage the relationship in a positive and proactive way (Lawson 2008). Ways of doing this will now be discussed.

Learning to Read your Supervisor

Experienced students recommend that you learn how your supervisor communicates, for example learn to read when he/she is busy, and learn to read when you can talk to him/her. Be observant but also be confident to check and ask for clarification if you have not really understood something .You will be spending a lot of time together and it is important to establish a comfortable and transparent relationship.

Manage the Relationship

In practical terms you also need to think about how to manage the relationship. It is essential to plan short term:

- Write a plan for your meetings (for example how often you will meet).
- Work out a meeting structure and a form to record issues discussed and action decided.
- Send an email to your supervisor after the meeting with a synopsis of what you discussed.

And plan long term:

- Work out a long term plan of how you will review writing over the life of your thesis. Find out when your supervisor will read your work and how long you can expect to wait before he/she returns your work.

Communication

It is vital that you keep your supervisor informed of what you are doing. For example:

- progress you are making;
- any problems or unexpected issues that you may be encountering;
- when you are going to meet.

Always be open, and seek clarification when necessary.

If problems arise (for example you may have problems with equipment or you may feel you have been waiting too long for feedback about something you have written), you need to state clearly and politely what you need. Remember that meetings may have to be short and may seem time-pressured. This does not mean your supervisor is not interested in you and your work. Becker and Denicolo (2008), suggest taking time after a meeting to think back carefully about what has been said and add points to your notes, and then consider emailing a synopsis of the meeting to your supervisor.

Suggestions

In a face-to-face meeting:
- Think ahead and before a meeting prepare questions that are as clear as possible
- Make sure to ask reasonable and thought through questions
- Learn to see when they have understood you and when you need to give more information
- When you don't understand, sit back for a minute, let it sink in a little then ask questions directly to clarify
- Be comfortable saying you don't understand.
  (Doctoral student in science, in Lawson 2008)

After the meeting or phone call:

Email your supervisor a summary of your meeting:
- restate what you discussed;
- give details of any research literature you discussed;

- confirm dates of meetings, conferences, key dates for your work;
- confirm actions taken and future plans.

Consider devising a template for these post-meeting summaries. Ask your supervisor if he/she is happy for you to do this, and how long is a reasonable time to wait for a reply (Becker and Denicolo 2008). The following phrases may help smooth the communication process.

Useful phrases for clarification

- I'm sorry, I didn't really catch that idea/comment/argument. Could you please explain it again?
- Is there anything I can read that will help me to understand this better?

Email Asking for a Change of Appointment

Dear [first name or title as appropriate]

Thank you for your help in our last meeting. I have attached my summary of the meeting for your information.
I'm sorry I have to change our next meeting. Would it be possible to meet you on . . .
I wonder when would be a good time for you to meet me/give me some feedback on chapter 2.

Thank you
Mia

STARTING YOUR RESEARCH: DEFINING AND SCOPING YOUR TOPIC

In order to define your topic you will need to read broadly and deeply in the subject area. As Stevens and Asmar (1999) note, a good thesis topic is narrow and deep. Learn to be critical of what you read. Go to library workshops to develop your literature searching skills and be informed by the supervisor on important authors to read. Allow the literature to shape every aspect of your proposal, theoretical framework and methodology.

Read other theses from the following online resources:

- http://www.ndltd.org/ – Global digital thesis collection.
- http://adt.caul.edu.au/ – Australian thesis collection.

- http://ethos.bl.uk/Home.do – British Library Electronic Thesis Online Service.
- http://www.dart-europe.eu/basic-search.php – European thesis online.

WRITING A THESIS IN A SECOND LANGUAGE

You Learn to Write by Writing

For most research students writing is a challenge, and if you are writing in your second language it is even more so. You will have passed the entry requirements, for example by sitting the IELTS (International English Language Testing System) test, but the difference between writing a short essay and a document of many thousand words is immense. Many students ask themselves how they can possibly write 300 pages. However for many international students the experience of writing during a research degree, while difficult, is an invaluable opportunity to learn to write fluent, professional English. This is a real advantage in many research fields as the majority of publications and conferences are in the English language.

Professor David Thambiratnam, a professor in civil engineering, himself once an international student and now a successful supervisor of many international research students, gave the following example. A Chinese engineer went to Australia to undertake doctoral research on bridge construction. He struggled with his writing, finding it hard even to summarize his own research ideas for his proposal. However with persistence, commitment and hard work over three years, he now writes fluently in English and has had a number of papers published in prestigious journals (cited in Lawson 2008).

Write Early and Regularly

A key to success that appears in many guides to writing a thesis is the need to write all the way through your research journey and not just leave writing until the last year. Successful development of writing needs practice. Writing regularly in a research log in English is a very valuable way to do this. Write about what you have been reading: for example make a habit of writing a paragraph in English when you finish reading each journal article or each chapter. This could be a summary, paraphrase or critical reflection. This will provide you with a rich resource tool that documents your work for future reference. Reading will also inform the writing process; you can improve your style by observing for example how published authors introduce the literature and justify their methodology.

Writing regularly like this will build your skills and your confidence. These notes will also be a valuable resource when it comes to writing your thesis and discussing topics with your supervisor. Also write up and date notes from meetings with your supervisor.

It's not enough to say, 'I need to write more'. Rowena Murray (2002) suggests making very specific writing goals. For example:

Not Do five minutes' writing practice every day
but
Do five minutes' writing practice today at 9.45
Not Make some notes on reading
but
Summarize and evaluate the paper I read yesterday
(500 words), spend 30 minutes

What Do I Need to Write?

The formal written requirements will differ between institutions and the degree being undertaken. You will be required to write a range of documents including a research proposal, a literature review and your final thesis. Check carefully what your institution requires and how this will be assessed.

The Proposal

This will normally need to be written in the first six months of your candidature (in some cases even after three months). A proposal is needed if you are going to do a research degree.

In this document you will be expected to provide an overview of your research idea, including an introduction and a statement of the research problem and the research question you will address. You will need to conduct a preliminary review of the literature which should enable you to establish the unique contribution your research will make. It should explore possible theoretical frameworks that will inform your research. The proposal will include some ideas about your proposed methodology, the proposed time line for your research and, above all, a sense of the unique contribution that your research will make to the field and its significance. Essentially the proposal aims to persuade the university that your research will make a valuable contribution to the field. See Punch (2006) for further information about writing effective research proposals.

In preparing your proposal use the following checklist and consider asking a colleague to give you feedback as well. At the end of the chapter there is a checklist that will help you to work with others to improve your writing. The research proposal will have a particular format and name depending on your institution. The main aim of the document is to present your research idea and supporting evidence in clear language in a way that will convince your faculty that your research is worth doing. Read your faculty guidelines carefully.

The proposal usually includes:

- The proposed title.
- A summary of the proposed research.
- Outline of research area and research problem.
- Aims and objectives.
- Literature review.
- Proposed methodology (may be quite tentative).
- Expected outcomes and significance of the research.
- Possible limitations and problems.
- Ethical and safety issues.
- References.

Thesis or Dissertation

A thesis is required for most honours, masters and doctoral degrees. It is a lengthy document (ranging from 10 000 words in an honours thesis to up to 80 000 words in a PhD thesis).

Typical elements of a thesis include:

- Abstract.
- Introduction.
- Literature review.
- Methodology.
- Results.
- Discussion.
- Conclusion.
- References.

However there is considerable variation in these elements, particularly if you are undertaking qualitative research.

Feedback

You will usually need to write many revisions of your work and to repeat some experiments. The feedback you receive from your supervisor and peers will be very important in helping you to produce quality research and a well written thesis.

Learn to be specific in the feedback you request:

Not: 'Please give me some feedback on Chapter 2.'
Rather ask: 'Have I organized the literature well? Is my writing analytical enough? Is the topic more focused? Do I link ideas?' (Adapted from Murray 2002)

Coping with feedback can sometimes be a challenge. You need to think ahead and prepare yourself for it. Sometimes a supervisor's comments may be very blunt and this can be upsetting. One doctoral student commented on the strategy she used to cope with this:

> First, I took all the comments (that were in red ink) and made them green, I changed statements like 'this is wrong' to 'this is incorrect and needs revising'; then I set about addressing the issues raised by my supervisor in a calm frame of mind. (Doctoral student in science)

Editing Strategy

It is vital that you learn how to read your own work critically. One useful way to do this is to use a three levels of edit approach.

Level 1:
- Re-read the faculty guidelines.
- Have you followed these?
- Re-read any feedback from your supervisor. Have you incorporated this?

Level 2:
- Think about the purpose of the document (for example a particular chapter).
- How clear are you?
- Use the writing circle checklist at the end of this chapter as a guide.

Level 3(1):
- Switch off your phone and make sure you will not be interrupted.
- Read for flow.
- Do paragraphs connect?
- Is there one main idea in each paragraph?
- Are sentences longer than three lines necessary?
- Does it make sense? Is it logical?

- Are connecting words logical?
- Are connecting words necessary?

Level 3 (2):
- Take a ruler (or digital equivalent) and go through line by line.
- Are references correctly formatted?
- Check for spelling mistakes.
- Check for grammatical errors (see 'Common errors' section at the end of Chapter 9 on writing).

You should also check with your university to see what kind of support is available, to help you develop your writing skills and to help you with editing and learning to edit your own work. If you are very unsure about your language, for the final draft of your thesis consider using a professional proofreading service. Your faculty should be able to provide you with information about this.

SPEAKING

As a research student there are a number of formal situations in which you will need to speak. These include:

- meetings with your supervisor;
- presentations of your work at team meetings;
- formal presentations at key stages of your research.

The formal presentation will involve the most work.

Formal Presentations

In most cases you will have a long presentation of your work (sometimes called a 'defence') at the end of your degree. This will be assessed and you will be questioned by a panel and possibly by the audience.

It is thus important to know your audience and tailor your presentation for them. Usually your audience will be academic, but if you have an industry sponsor you need to consider what kind of questions they may ask and what parts of your presentation they will need clarification on.

The following suggestions will help you prepare for a formal presentation:

- Write out your presentation but do not read it.
- Keep the structure clear and as simple as possible.

- Use an appropriate number of PowerPoint slides for the length of your presentation.
- Make sure these are written in clear professional English (do not excessively cut and paste from your thesis).
- Pause after important points.
- Pay special attention to include signal words, for example 'Having considered X now let's look at Y'. Pause and emphasize these words.
- Spread eye contact evenly across the room. Avoid nervous mannerisms.
- Prepare well for questions.
- Practice as often as you can by yourself (perhaps film yourself or use a mirror) and with friends, family and colleagues. Research suggests that practice with friends and colleagues is particularly useful in promoting self-efficacy in research seminar presentations (Adams 2004).

You will find further information on presentation skills in Chapter 10.

COMMUNICATION WITH YOUR COLLEAGUES

If you are researching in a second language it can be a challenge to develop and maintain your communication skills when you are reading and doing research for so many hours a day. Take every opportunity to attend seminars, training courses and even social functions held in your school or department. It is important also to relate well to fellow team members; it may seem that you have no time to have lunch and coffee breaks with them, but ultimately your research life will be enhanced if you have good working relationships with those around you. Also get to know and chat with technical and administrative staff; they will be of great assistance.

PERSONAL STRENGTH AND RESILIENCE

> Learn how to encourage yourself and sometimes rescue yourself. Don't always stay in your room. You will be alone. Don't panic, learn to be alone, learn how to rescue yourself. (Chinese doctoral student, in Lawson 2008)

A number of studies have shown that personal resilience is a key factor in succeeding in postgraduate studies (Wright and Cochrane 2000; Wang 2009). Resilience involves being successful despite challenging circumstances. As an international graduate student you are likely already to have strong levels of resilience and perseverance and you will need to use all these strengths in your study. There are many parallels between challenges you are facing and those faced by expatriate managers. Research on factors associated with successful global practice found the following factors to be crucial:

- good communication skills;
- stress tolerance;
- tolerance of ambiguity and patience.

Good Communication Skills

What strategies can you put in place to develop these? Check out extra language programmes, conversation groups and make use of radio and television programmes in your discipline area. For example these radio programmes have transcripts which can be very helpful in developing confidence:

- Law: http://www.abc.net.au/rn/lawreport/.
- Science: http://www.abc.net.au/rn/scienceshow/default.htm.
- Medicine: http://www.abc.net.au/rn/healthreport/.

Stress Tolerance

Make sure to develop a good network of social support. Consider forming a group that meets regularly to discuss how things are going. Check out the postgraduate student associations at your university for events where you can meet people. It's also good to have time out with friends from your own country.

Keeping a healthy work–life balance, getting enough sleep, exercising regularly, alone and with others, and eating good food, will also be vital in helping you deal with stress.

Planning your time well and avoiding procrastination are among the best ways to handle stress. Set yourself weekly goals and then break these into smaller daily goals. Then reward yourself for achieving these goals. When you have had a setback, learn how to pick yourself up, encourage yourself and start again with fresh purpose.

Tolerance of Ambiguity and Patience

It's hard sometime to realise that part of doing a PhD is that you are discovering something new and that means that it will be uncertain and you don't have to have all the answers, but it's about working through that. (Professor Patsy Yates, in Lawson, 2008)

There will be times in your daily life in a foreign country where you will simply need to accept that you don't quite know how the system works and you have to give yourself time to understand. Be patient if you are faced with bureaucratic delays: universities are large organizations with administrative systems that may be very different to the ones you are used to dealing with. But don't suffer in silence. Look after your health. Talk to those around you and staff in your faculty.

Likewise in your research there will be times of great uncertainty. Working through these times, discussing issues with your supervisor and colleagues, and doing further reading will all help to deepen your knowledge of your area.

Note how this successful doctoral student in life sciences was able to redirect herself despite a number of setbacks in the lab. She lists her priorities, she plans her time very concretely, she talks to others and encourages herself on the research journey:

> Am trying to keep on top of things . . . making priorities is the big thing. I am working at getting in regular discipline with exercise . . . because my body/mind is so tired and fatigued at end of every day.
>
> Was able to work with one of the research assistants who is using the method I need to use for my new plan of experiments. That was good . . . worked through the details last night. Today I am catching up with 'postponed priorities' which didn't fit in this week. I went to the Glasshouse Mountains last Friday and looked at the plants I need to use. Will be going back on Monday morning to collect samples.
>
> My plan this weekend is to read and write the literature around this plan of experiments. Then I can begin the analysis next week.

Passion for Your Research

Passion for your research will keep you going through such difficult stages in the research process. If you are passionate about your research, your supervisors will enjoy supervising you. Keep your passion for your research alive by reading widely and keeping abreast of the latest publications through electronic feeds and by talking to the librarian who is a specialist in your field. Attend conferences and seminars and present your work whenever you are given an opportunity. Look for opportunities to attend your colleagues' seminars and presentations.

WRITING CHECKLIST

This checklist can be used to help you edit your work; in this case, an abstract. You could use the same list with other sections of your work. You could also ask a colleague to give you feedback using this sheet.

Take your abstract. Comment on its clarity and structure. Do not comment on language, grammar or spelling until you have done this!

	Clear	Could be clearer
1. In terms of structure, is the abstract easy to follow?	○	○
2. Is the topic of the research clear? Give example if something is confusing.	○	○
3. Is the gap in existing knowledge base clearly identified? What could be clearer?	○	○
4. Is methodology clear? If yes, what is it? What could be clearer?	○	○
5. Are the outcomes of the research clearly stated? Give example	○	○
6. Do you get a sense of the significance of the research? Give example	○	○

Read again: now give any useful feedback on language, grammar, spelling, incomplete sentences.

Find an abstract from a field you are interested in researching. Read the abstract using the above checklist. How clear is it?

NOTE

* The authors would like to thank the many international doctoral students at Queensland University of Technology who have shared their experiences and stories with the authors and contributed directly and indirectly to this chapter.

REFERENCES AND FURTHER READING

Adams, K. (2004), 'Modelling success: enhancing international post graduate research students, self efficacy for research seminar presentations', *Higher Education Research and Development*, **23** (2), 116–30.

Becker, L. and P. Denicolo (2008), 'Managing the research process and the supervisory relationship', in G. Hall and J. Longman (eds), *The Postgraduate's Companion*, London: Sage, pp. 143–61.

Bound, J., S. Turner and P. Walsh (2009), 'Internationalization of US doctorate education', National Bureau of Economic Research Working Paper No. 14792.

Bryce, M. (2003), 'Defining the doctorate with the Asian student', paper presented at Newcastle Mini Conference of the Association of Active Educational Research; http://www.aare.edu.au/conf03nc/br03015z.pdf. Accessed 11 March 2010.

Denholm, C. and T. Evans (eds) (2006), *Doctorates Down Under: Keys to Successful Doctoral Study in Australia and New Zealand*, Melbourne: ACER.

European Commission (2009), 'ERA indicators and monitoring', ftp://ftp.cordis. europa.eu/pub/era/docs/era_indicators&monitoring.pdf. Accessed 8 March 2010.

Hall, G. and J. Longman (eds) (2008), *The Postgraduate's Companion*, London: Sage.

Humphrey, R. and P. McCarthy (1999), 'Recognising difference: providing for post graduate students', *Studies in Higher Education*, **24**, 371–86.

Jackson, T. (ed.) (1995), *Cross-Cultural Management*, Oxford: Butterworth Heinemann.

Lawson, L. (2008), *International HDR Students and their Supervisors* (DVD), Brisbane: QUT.

Moses, I. (1992), 'Research training in Australian universities – undergraduate and graduate studies', in O. Zuber-Skerritt (ed.), *Starting Research – Supervision and Training*, Brisbane: Tertiary Education Institute, pp. 4–6.

Murray, R. (2002), *How to Write a Thesis*, Maidenhead: Open University Press.

Paltridge, B. and S. Starfield (2007), *Thesis and Dissertation Writing in a Second Language: A Handbook for Supervisors*, London: Routledge.

Powell, S. and H. Green (2008), 'What is a postgraduate degree?' in G. Hall and J. Longman (eds), *The Postgraduate's Companion*, London: Sage, pp. 6–34.

Punch, K. (2000), *Effective Proposals*, London: Sage.

Punch, K. (2006), *Developing Effective Research Proposals*, Thousand Oaks, CA: Sage.

Sinclair, M. (2005), 'The pedagogy of "good" PhD supervision: a national cross-disciplinary investigation of PhD supervision', http://www.dest.gov.au/sectors/

higher_education/publications_resources/profiles/pedagogy_of_good_phd_supervision.htm. Accessed 13 March 2010.

Stevens, K. and C. Asmar (1999), *Doing Postgraduate Research in Australia*, Melbourne: Melbourne University Press.

Wang, J. (2009), 'A study of resiliency characteristics of international graduate students at American universities', *Journal of Studies in International Education*, **13** (1), 22–45.

Wright, T. and R. Cochrane (2000), 'Factors influencing successful submission of PhD theses', *Studies in Higher Education*, **25** (20), 181–95.

Resources

Information on Australian scholarships and other information about being a student in Australia can be found at: http://www.students.idp.com/education_system/scholarships.aspx.

The Council of Graduate Schools offers advice and sources of funding for prospective graduate students to USA and Canada. www.cgsnet.org/.

Education UK provides links for all aspects of postgraduate study in the UK: www.educationuk.org.

The European Research Council provides information about research grants in the European Union: http://erc.europa.eu/.

For information about study in the USA, this site provides a good place to start: http://educationusa.state.gov/.

Index

academic credit 23
academic style 110, 126–7
accommodation 24–5, 34
Adams, K. 161
analysis
  business case 100, 102
  case teaching method 81, 84, 143–4
  and communication, written 102,
    103, 104
Anderson, M. 48
Asmar, C. 155
assessment and examination success
  applied workplace projects 145–6
  assessment definition 135–6
  assessment purpose 136, 137–40
  assessment types 139–47
  assignment tips 142–3
  assignments and essay writing 97,
    98, 99, 106–7, 110–14, 142
  authentic assessment 137–8
  case examinations 92–3
  and case study analysis 86, 143–4
  course grades, and case teaching
    method 86
  criterion-referenced and norm-
    referenced assessment 138
  examination tips 141
  examination types 140
  formative and summative
    assessment 136–8
  grading and marking, and
    communication, written
    101–2
  group assessment 146–7
  and group work 27
  oral examinations 144–5
  and plagiarism 142, 147
  research assessment 101–2, 160–61,
    162
Australia 2, 36
Avirutha, A. 2, 3

Ballard, B. 16, 17, 135
Barber, P. 70
Barnes, D. 48
Barribal, L. 21
Beaver, D. 52
Becker, L. 154, 155
Biggs, J. 49, 59, 136
Blevins, D. 48
Bligh, D. 49, 70
Bloom, J. 83–4
Bloom's Taxonomy guidelines
    139–40
  see also case teaching method
Bonwell, C. 80
Bound, J. 149
Bremer, D. 32
Brislin, R. 39
Budner, S. 41
Burns, T. 131
business environment *see* workplace

Canada 2, 37
case teaching method 80–95
  analytical skills 81, 84, 143–4
  application skills 82
  assessment and examination success
    86, 92–3, 143–4
  benefits of 88–90
  Bloom's Taxonomy guidelines
    139–40
  case reports 92
  cognitive learning objectives
    83–4
  conceptual dimension 84
  and confidence building 86
  and course grades 86
  creative skills 82
  and cultural practices 89–90, 94
  decision-making skills 82
  discussion phases 89
  good practice guidelines 93–4

instructor's role 89
interpersonal and social skills 82
large group discussion 86, 90–91
learning process 84–5
learning process management 93–4
long-cycle preparation process
    87–8
oral communication skills 82, 85,
    86
overview 80–81
and participation confidence and
    effectiveness 86, 87–8
participation enhancement 88–90
participation problems, overcoming
    90–91
popularity of 83–4
and preparation 85, 86, 87–8, 90
presentation dimension 84–5
presentation feedback 91
short-cycle preparation process 87
skills involved 81–2
small group discussion, importance
    of 85–6
student role 84
and teamwork 86
time management skills 82
written communication skills 82
certification for study 22
see also exchange and study abroad
Chapman, A. 6
Chislett, V. 6
Christensen, C. 83, 89
Clanchy, J. 16, 17, 135
Clemens, D. 70
Cochrane, R. 150, 161
communication, spoken
    academic style 126–7
    body language and pace 124
    and case teaching method 82, 85, 86
    challenges and performance
        improvement 120–23
    and cultural differences 121, 122
    importance of 119–20
    and international education 17–18
    and language problems 121–2
    language for tutorial participation
        132
    learning from others 124
    lectures and language difficulties 51,
        55

and participation 61, 62, 65, 67, 124
and preparation 120
presentation *see* presentation
research education *see* research
    education
success strategies 123–5
and tutor expectations 123–4
and tutorials 122–3, 132
and understanding of topics 120
useful resources 134
and written language, differences
    between 125–6
communication, written
    academic style 110, 126–7
    and analysis 102, 103, 104
    argument, definition of 103
    business case analysis 100, 102
    case study reports 92
    common problems 108–10
    content marking 101
    cultural differences and study 44–6
    descriptive writing 103–4
    editing skills 159–60, 164–5
    essay time plan 106–7
    essay writing 97, 98, 99, 106–7,
        110–14
    flow problems 108–9
    grading and marking 101–2
    grammatical errors 116–17
    improvement of 105–6
    and language deficiencies 105,
        116–17
    learning advice services 106
    literature review, relevant 97–8,
        102
    online discussion 100
    oral presentations, research
        education 160–61, 162
    paragraph length and organization
        109
    paraphrasing work of other authors
        108
    and plagiarism 107–8
    presentaton and accuracy 102
    professional documents 101
    proofreading and common errors
        116–17
    reading skills, improving 106–7
    referencing work 107
    reflective journal 100–101

report writing 98–9, 102
reporting verbs 115–16
research education *see* research
  education
resources, useful 115–17, 118
and spoken language, differences
  between 125–6
and structure 102
and style 109–10
subject matter 96–101
thesis 100, 103
websites, useful 118
confidence building 20–21, 86
  see also personal attributes
copying (plagiarism) 107–8, 142, 147
cultural differences and study
  adjustments to, and ambiguity 41–3,
    44
  and case teaching method 89–90, 94
  challenges of 23, 29
  and communication, spoken 121,
    122
  competency advice 44
  and core assumptions 11–12
  cross-cultural communication 44–6
  and cultural empathy 44
  culture, definition of 10–11
  culture shock 39–40
  English accents 45
  groups and teams, working in 72, 73,
    74, 77–8
  impact of 10–12
  language problems 44–6
  misattribution of observed
    behaviour 46
  and participation 60–61, 64, 65
  and research supervision 153
  and returning home 46–7
  student reflections 40–41

Danowitz Sagaria, M. 3
De Cieri, H. 3
Denicolo, P. 154, 155
Dessoff, A. 32
disabled students 32
Duncan, C. 136

editing skills 159–60, 164–5
  see also communication, written
Eison, J. 80

essay writing 97, 98, 99, 106–7, 110–14,
    142
  see also assessment and examination
    success; communication,
    written
EU 2, 20, 24, 36–7, 149
Evans, P. 17, 143–4
examination success *see* assessment
    and examination success
exchange and study abroad 20–37
  and academic credit 23
  accommodation 24–5, 34
  adjustment to 26–30
  certification 22
  checklist 33–5
  confidence as global student 20–21
  cultural challenges 23, 29
  emotional challenges 27–9, 30–31
  exams and group work 27
  financial considerations 23–4, 25, 33
  and future career 21–2
  guide book, personal 25–6
  health issues 25, 34
  health and safety 30
  internships 31–2
  online pre-departure training course
    26
  and open-mindedness 24
  period of study 23
  preparation for 24–6, 33–5
  reasons for 20
  and returning home 30–31
  study decisions 22–4, 35
  visas and passports 24, 33
  websites, useful 26, 36–7
  see also international eduaction

financial considerations 23–4, 25, 33
Fowler, B. 139
France 37
Frenkel-Brunswick, E. 44
Frey, B. 137
Furnham, A. 39–40
future career 21–2

Gallagher, J. 73
Gillespie, J. 21, 22
Glasser, W. 59
grading *see* assessment and
    examination success

grammatical errors 116–17
  see also communication, written
Green, H. 149
Griffiths, S. 70
groups and teams, working in
  and assessment and examination
    success 146–7
  benefits of 70, 76
  and case teaching method 85–6,
    90–91
  cognitive constructivism approach
    72–3
  conflict resolution 78
  cultural differences 72, 73, 74,
    77–8
  freeloading and size of group 75
  group formation 75–6
  group potential, identifying 77
  and group size 74–5
  and human element 73–4
  individual roles 76
  long-term group work 73–4
  problem resolving 76–7
  short-term group work 72–3
  work practice discussion 76
  workplace group work comparison
    71–2
Gulikers, J. 136, 137

Hadis, B. 21, 24
Hamilton, L. 104
Hampden-Turner, C. 8, 10, 12
Hancock, M. 134
health issues 25, 34
health and safety 30
Holmes, H. 45
Humphrey, R. 153

instructor's role *see* tutorials
international education
  achievement versus ascription 15
  advantages of 3–4
  challenges of 4–5
  communitarianism versus
    individualism 13–14
  diffuse versus specific 14
  language and communication
    17–18
  learning process, understanding
    5–7

neutral versus emotional 14
  teachers, relationships with 16–17
  teaching and learning expectations
    15–16
  universalism versus particularism
    13
  see also exchange and study abroad
internships 31–2
Ireland 37

Johnson, D. 70
Jones, L. 4

Kean, T. 104
Kjellen, B. 80
Kluckhohn, F. 12
Knight, J. 3

Ladika, S. 32
language problems *see* communication,
    spoken; communication, written
Lawson, L. 96, 150, 153, 154, 156, 161,
    163
Leach, L. 48
learning advice services 105
  see also resources
learning from others 64–5, 124
learning process 84–5, 93–4
  Bloom's Taxonomy guidelines
    139–40
  visual–auditory–kinaesthetic
    learning style model (VAK) 5–7
lectures
  benefiting from 48–57
  challenging lecturer 50–51
  concentration, maintaining 52
  expectations, shared 50, 53–4
  functions of good 49
  good practice checklist 56
  humour, use of 52
  and individual viewpoints, differing
    50
  and language difficulties 51–2, 55
  lecturer's perspective on
    participation 66–7
  limitations of 48–50
  loneliness, feelings of 54
  and participation *see* participation
  preparation, benefits of 55, 56
  recording 55

rules and procedures 52–3
and student engagement 55–6
see also tutorials
Leggett, K. 32
Lobel, S. 44
loneliness, feelings of 54
see also personal attributes
Loveland, E. 20

McCann, D. 77
McCarthy, P. 153
Mcormack, K. 21
Margerison, C. 77
Marginson, S. 2
Marshall, L. 49, 141
Mauffette-Leenders, L. 81–2, 87, 143–4
Mehrabian, A. 128–9
Merseth, K. 83
Moore, D. 48
Moses, I. 152
Murray, R. 157, 159

Nastasi, B. 70
Netherlands 37
New Zealand 2
Noonan, B. 136
Norris, E. 21, 22

Oberg, K. 39
Olekalns, M. 3
oral examinations and presentations
144–5, 160–61, 162
see also assessment and examination
success; communication,
spoken

Paltridge, B. 152
participation
anxiety associated with 61, 65
benefits of 58–61
and case teaching method 86, 87–91
challenges and skills 58–69
checklist 68
cultural differences 60–61, 64, 65
and expectations, personal and
shared 62–3
and language problems 61, 62, 65,
67
learning environment, comfortable
63–5

lecturer's perspective on 66–7
and pairing with other student 64–5
and postgraduate studies 60
and preparation 62–3, 66
problems 61–2
and self-confidence 64, 65
and self-image 60
and shared experiences 59–60,
63–4
personal attributes
and emotional challenges 27–9
interpersonal and social skills 82
patience and tolerance development
162–3
self-confidence 64, 65
self-image 60
strength and resilience 161–3
stress, coping with 162
Petress, K. 58, 67
Pincas, A. 4
plagiarism 108, 142, 147
postgraduate studies *see* research
education
Powell, S. 149
preparation
and case teaching method 85, 86,
87–8, 90
and communication, spoken 120
for exchange and study abroad 24–6,
33–5
and lectures 55, 56
and participation 62–3, 66
presentation
and case teaching method 84–5, 91
delivery 129–30
improvements 131
language 132–3
and non-verbal communication
129
oral, and research education 160–61,
162
preparation 128–9
skills 125–31
structure 127–8
and written accuracy 102
see also communication, spoken
proofreading and common errors
116–17
see also communication, written
Punch, K. 157

Race, P. 73, 74
reading skills, improving 106–7
  see also communication, written
referencing work 107
  see also communication, written
Reid, D. 73
report writing 92, 98–9, 102
  see also communication, written
research education
  assessment 101–2
  editing skills 159–60, 164–5
  globalization of 149–50
  oral presentations 160–61, 162
  and participation 60
  patience and tolerance development
    162–3
  personal strength and resilience
    161–3
  proposal, written 100, 157–8
  and research expectations 150–51
  and research passion 163
  research topic, defining and scoping
    155–6
  stress, coping with 162
  thesis online resources 155–6
  thesis requirements 158
  useful resource websites 162, 166
  and writing practice 156–7
  and writing in a second language
    156–60
  see also communication, spoken;
    communication, written
research supervision
  communication strategies 154–5
  and cultural differences 153
  feedback 158–9
  management of 153–4
  relationship 151–5
relationship assessment form 152
resources, useful
  communication, spoken 134
  communication, written 115–17,
    118
  exchange and study abroad 26,
    36–7
  and internships 31–2
  learning advice services 106
  online pre-departure training course
    26
returning home 30–31, 46–7

Rhee, J. 3
Rowland F. 49, 141
Rubin, K. 31
Ryan, J. 48, 61, 62, 135

Schein, E. 10
Schmitt, V. 137
Sinclair, M. 152
Sinfield, S. 131
Sivan, A. 80
Slavin, R. 70
Smith, M. 48
spoken communication *see*
  communication, spoken
Starfield, S. 152
Stenhouse, L. 70
Stevens, K. 155
stress, coping with 162
Strodtbeck, F. 12
study decisions 22–4, 35
Sweden 37

Tangtongtavy, S. 45
teachers *see* tutorials
teamwork *see* groups and teams,
  working in
Thambiratnam, D. 156
thesis 100
  and argument 103
  online resources 155–6
  requirements 158
  see also assessment and
    examination success;
    communication, spoken;
    communication, written;
    research education
time management skills 82, 105
Tobenkin, D. 22
Triandis, H. 12
Trompenaars, A. 7, 10, 12
tutorials
  case teaching method 89
  and communication, spoken 122–3,
    131–2
  tutor expectations 15–16, 123–4
  tutors, relationships with 16–17
  see also lectures

UK 2, 36–7, 149
USA 1–2, 20, 32, 37, 149

visas and passports 24, 33
visual–auditory–kinaesthetic learning
   style model (VAK) 5–7

Wang, J. 161
websites *see* resources, useful
Weimer, M. 55
workplace
  applied workplace projects 145–6
  business case analysis 100, 102

group work comparison 71–2
  internships 31–2
Wright, T. 150, 161
written communication *see*
  communication, written

Yates, P. 150, 163
Yoshida, T. 39

Zepke, N. 48